They Pu

Our House

Down

The Story of Baswich House
and its People

Arms of Thomas Salt Esq. of Weeping Cross, Stafford.

Dedicated
to the memory of

RICHARD CHARLES PEPPER

1929 – 2009

Richard was a founder member
of Berkswich History Society.
He gave freely of his time over the years as
Treasurer, Chairman and President

ISBN 978-0-9527247-6-6
Copyright Berkswich History Society
Printed by Titus Wilson & Son, Kendal

**This book has been researched and compiled
by Members of Berkswich History Society
2009**

Cover painting.
Sarah, Harriet and Thomas Salt,
Children of Thomas Salt Esq. of Weeping Cross, Stafford
by T. Barber, 1838

Reproduced by kind permission of
Sir Michael Salt. Bt.

Contents

Page

Foreword by Sir Michael Salt

Introduction

Appendices

Abbreviations

BA   Birmingham Archives at Birmingham Museum and Art Gallery
SRO   Staffordshire Record Office, Eastgate Street, Stafford
WA   Wolverhampton Archives, Molineux Hotel Building, Wolverhampton
WSL   William Salt Library, Eastgate Street, Stafford

Foreword

By Sir T. Michael J. Salt,

4th Baronet of Standon and Weeping Cross, in the County of Stafford.

I was very pleased to be asked by Beryl Holt, Chairman of Berkswich History Society, to write a foreword for this history of Baswich House, or Weeping Cross House, as I knew it, which was built by my great great grandfather in the mid nineteenth century.

I much enjoyed the first three-quarters of the book, but the latter chapters made somewhat distressing reading. I regard fine old houses as similar to fine old trees; irreplaceable and to be retained at all cost. Sadly this sentiment was not shared by certain factions in Staffordshire, and Weeping Cross House is no more.

I commend all those who fought to save the house and especially Berkswich History Society for this excellent history which has, I know, taken members to all corners of the country in their search for information about the house and those who lived in it.

Michael Salt,
Dorset.

December 2009

They Pulled our House Down
The Story of Baswich House and its People

Introduction

During March 2009, a large red brick house, originally called "Weeping Cross House" but more recently known as "Baswich House", was demolished by Staffordshire Police Authority. It may be worth recording at this point, that the home of the Salt family was known as "Weeping Cross House" until 1915 when it became "Baswich House School". The Twigg family lived in a house on the opposite side of the Cannock Road that also became known as "Weeping Cross House". The "Twigg" house was demolished in the 1960's along with Barnfields Farm, to allow housing development at Wildwood.

Local residents were totally opposed to the demolition of Baswich House, but all attempts to stop the destruction failed. For many years the house was the home of the Salt family who had a great influence over the development of Stafford for almost a century. Local people, including those who worked on this book, knew very little of the family that was so involved with the town. The Salts were the motivators for building a new grammar school; they donated substantial funds towards the construction of several Staffordshire churches, provided a Chairman of Lloyds Bank, ensured the existence of the William Salt Library and worked in the town to make the lot of the poor a little more bearable. In conveying the story of this family we have sometimes drifted away from Baswich House to tell you about their lives. We hope you will forgive us for this. There are many aspects of the lives of Thomas Senior and Thomas Junior that we have only touched upon. To completely record their lives would take many, many hours of research and we had to remember that this was a book about a house rather than about the first family who lived in it!

From time to time, we have found it difficult to untangle Thomas Salt Senior (1802 - 1871) from his son, Thomas Salt M.P. (1830 - 1904). Other authors have referred to the father as Sir Thomas Salt, when in fact it was his son who was Sir Thomas, and he did not receive his Baronetcy from Queen Victoria until 1899, just five years before his death. We hope that we have managed to credit their actions to the correct Thomas. To help unravel the various members of the family we have included a family tree at the back of the book. (Appendix 1)

This book, researched and written by members of Berkswich History Society, records as far as possible, the story of the Salt and Philips families and the history of the site at Weeping Cross, from 1800 until the final bricks were carted away on the back of a lorry in March 2009.

We uncovered the happy and the sad times experienced by those who lived in the house. We relived fêtes, weddings and funerals, fires and wartime memories. All these events help to tell the detailed story of two families, two schools and a Victorian house. Finally we go on to tell of the demise of the house in 2009.

Those who have worked on this book are all local people who have a love of the area in which they live and who are appalled at the actions of Staffordshire Police Authority in destroying our heritage.

Baswich House may have gone for ever but we hope that this book will help you remember what once was, and also record events which happened in Stafford well before any of us were born.

Beryl Holt,
Chairman,
Berkswich History Society,
2009

Chapter 1

The Salt Family come to Weeping Cross

"John Stevenson Salt of the Parish of St Clements Danes in the County of Middlesex, Bachelor and Sarah Stevenson of this Parish, Spinster and Minor, with consent of her Father was married in this church by Licence this seventh day of January in the year one thousand eight hundred by me Joseph Ellerton, Curate.
This marriage was solemnized between J.S. Salt
Sarah Stevenson
In the presence of Ann Stevenson, William Stevenson, S Stevenson"[1]

On Tuesday 7th January 1800, a young girl, not quite twenty, was to marry her cousin John Stevenson Salt Esq., of Lombard Street, London at Baswich Church. The groom was five years older than his bride, Sarah Stevenson, who, as she was not yet twenty-one, required the permission of her father, William Stevenson of Baswich, to marry.[2] William may have been reluctant to see his youngest daughter married, but John was a good catch by any standards and the couple had known each other all their lives as they had a common grandfather in John Stevenson. William and his nephew John Stevenson Salt were also in business together as bankers in London.

Baswich Church

Sarah's life was to change completely. Her mother had died when she was only two so she had little idea of what happy married life would be like and she would also be leaving behind her dear elder sister, Ann. Her journey to church along Baswich Lane, with open fields stretching into the distance in all directions reminded her that this would soon be lost and replaced by the bustle and noise of London.

---

[1] WSL D1716/5/7
[2] The age at which you were able to marry without parental consent was reduced from 21 to 18 in 1969

As John and Sarah travelled south on their honeymoon the story goes that they were robbed by highwaymen, as they neared Maidenhead Thicket. Not a good start to married life![3]

Maybe the family were unlucky to be robbed twice, or perhaps with the passing of time events became confused, but a report in the Staffordshire Advertiser on 28th September 1799 tells how William Stevenson and his daughter were, on 13th September, stopped in their post chaise near East Barnet by two highwaymen with masks over their faces. They were robbed of two watches and £10 in cash. This event occurred just four months before the wedding.

Following their honeymoon, the newly weds returned to live in Camden Town and before the year was out their first child, Mary was born. Mary was followed by Thomas in 1802, Sarah in 1803, Elizabeth 1804, John 1806, Maria 1807, William 1808, Joseph 1810, Emma 1812, Harriett, 1814, George 1820, a stillborn son in 1823, and Samuel in 1824.

William was to become a great collector of anything to do with Staffordshire and, although he never lived in the county, it was his collection which formed the basis of the William Salt Library. More of that later, but it is the story of the eldest son Thomas and his family that we will relate in the early chapters of this book.

Little Maria lived only a short while and was buried in October 1807, in the Old Church, St Pancras, where her older brothers and sisters had been baptised. 1807 had been an unhappy year for the family as Sarah had lost her father on 14th February aged just 55. He died in Dulwich and it took 4 days to bring his body back to Stafford in a hearse drawn by six horses. The standard charge for "house room" for a corpse at an Inn overnight appears to have been two guineas. Sarah's father was buried with his parents in St Mary's Church, Stafford.

The White House formerly the Weeping Cross Inn

---

[3] WSL 208/202 Press Cutting dated 17th April 1909

In 1813 an opportunity arose for John to buy a family home in the Parish of Berkswich. The Weeping Cross Inn was for sale by auction.

Advertised by Wright & Son of Market Drayton, the auction took place at the Vine Inn, Stafford on Friday, 16th July, 1813. The property was described as "a large and substantial dwelling house with outbuildings, stables, cowhouses, summer-house, bowling-green, garden and other appurtenances. Lately occupied as an Inn and known by the sign of the Weeping Cross, containing together about four thousand square yards of excellent land, and several sittings in the Parish Church of Berkswich.

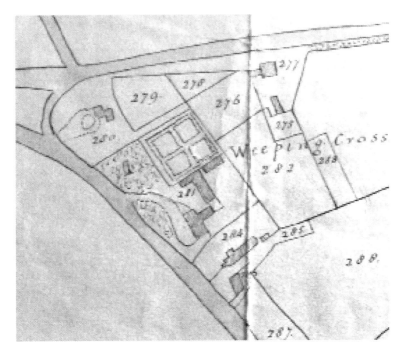

A Plan of Weeping Cross before the building of "Baswich House".

The numbers on the map relate to field names on the Parish Tithe Map. 279 & 280 belong to Elizabeth Ellerton. 281 is the White House, all remaining houses and land belong to the Salt family

These premises command, in front, a full west view of the ancient Borough of Stafford, Stafford Castle, Billington Bank, and numerous other beautiful objects: and in the ulterior, several delightful views of Staffordshire, Shropshire and Derbyshire, and are situated on an easy eminence, very dry and healthy, adjoining the great road from Stafford to Lichfield and one other to Birmingham: about two miles from Cannock Chase, in a very genteel neighbourhood, and at a light expense the premises may be converted into a desirable residence for a genteel family: therefore the auctioneers beg to decline any comment, more than to request the curious to view this charming spot. Possession may be had at Michaelmas next".[4]

We do not know whether competition for the Inn was keen, but John Stevenson Salt was successful in purchasing the property. He now had to turn it into a desirable residence for his wife and family. Once all the work on the house was complete it was renamed "The White House". The property was not very big. It must have been quite a squeeze for such a large family, although the boys were sent away to school from an early age. The family was soon well and truly settled at Weeping Cross.

Brocton Lodge, Brocton Nr. Stafford

On 12th August, 1829, Thomas the eldest son of John and Sarah, who was now twenty-seven, and well established as a banker in the family firm, married Harriet Letitia Petit, eldest daughter of the late Rev. John Hayes Petit, rector of Donnington, at Baswich Church. "The lovely bride was conducted to the altar by her uncle, Louis Hayes Petit, M.P., attended by numerous family members in the most elegant and superb dresses"[5] The ceremony was performed by the bride's brother Rev. John Louis Petit who, although he had taken Holy Orders, had never performed any parochial work. The Petits, descended from a Huguenot family from Normandy, all seem to have been talented artists. John Louis had a special interest in churches and church architecture, and spent much of his later life sketching scenes in Shropshire and Staffordshire.

---

[4] WSL D1716/16/21
[5] Staffordshire Advertiser 15th August 1829

After the wedding ceremony, the happy couple and their guests travelled to Brocton Lodge for "a most sumptuous and splendid entertainment" before leaving for a honeymoon in the Isle of Wight. Brocton Lodge was the home of the bride's sister Mary Ann who had married Henry Chetwynd just eighteen months earlier.

Rev John Louis Petit
Water colour artist

Maybe it had something to do with his son leaving the family home, but just a few days after the wedding John Stevenson Salt decided to request that the body of his infant daughter Maria, be removed from the Old Church, St Pancras and brought to be re-interred in the family vault in St Mary's, Stafford.

His appeal was granted "provided always that the said John Stevenson Salt does no damage whatsoever to the said Old Church of St Pancras."[6] The Old Church had been left to deteriorate following the erection of a new church in 1822.[7] As Maria's name does not appear on the family memorial in St Mary's Church, there is some doubt as to whether her body was in fact brought to Stafford.

Although he owned the house at Weeping Cross, John Stevenson Salt continued to spend most of his time in his house at 9 Russell Square, London, managing the London Branch of the family bank, thus allowing his son, Thomas, and his family to occupy "The White House", at Weeping Cross.

Just nine months after their marriage, Thomas and Harriet, became the proud parents of twins, born on 12th May, 1830. The babies, named Thomas and Harriet after their parents, were baptised at Baswich Church on 15th May.

January 1831 brought a touch of excitement to the area but not of an enjoyable kind. Burglars entered "The White House" through the kitchen window during the early hours of the morning, while the family slept upstairs. Not only did they remove valuable items, they also helped themselves to wine while systematically searching the house. Among the items stolen were silver forks and spoons, most of which were marked with a dove holding an olive branch, a symbol that was incorporated into the Salt coat of arms. Perhaps the most valuable items stolen were a rosewood clock with a gold dial and a miniature, set in gold, cyphered J.H.P., the initials of Harriet's father, John Hayes Petit.[8]

It is believed that the perpetrators of this crime were the same gang who had, just a few nights earlier, been responsible for the theft of poultry from Barnfields Farm, the home of Mr John Twigg, which was just a few yards away on the opposite side of the road to Cannock. The body of a distinctive cockerel, which had been

---

[6] WSL D1716/5
[7] By 1845 the Old Church was completely derelict. It has since been rebuilt and is now a Grade II* listed building.
[8] Staffordshire Advertiser 8th January, 1831.

stolen from Barnfields, had been thrown into a pit close to the Salt's house on the night of the robbery.

August 1831 saw the birth of a third child, who was baptised Sarah. An announcement in the Staffordshire Advertiser on 20th April 1833 tells of the birth of yet another daughter but this was not a happy time. The next edition of the Advertiser records the death "On Wednesday, 24th instant, Harriet Letitia, wife of Thomas Salt of Weeping Cross".

Barnfields Farm

Yet another week, and another edition of the newspaper and we see that Mary Ann, the infant daughter of Thomas Salt had survived her mother by just 4 days. Mother and daughter were buried together in St Mary's Church, Stafford. At the age of 31 Thomas was a widower with three children, Thomas, Harriet and Sarah. The twins were still not quite three.

In 1838 John was appointed High Sheriff of Staffordshire. Because of poor health he tried to refuse the honour but the powers that be would not hear of it. They did however agree to let his son, Thomas, perform the duties of High Sheriff at the Assizes on the 10th March, as his proxy.

John was a devout Christian and donated money freely for building a new Church, St Paul's, Forebridge, in the parish of Castle Church. He was due to lay the foundation stone for this church in July 1841 but was unwell. The task was therefore undertaken by his son Thomas, who had been involved with raising money for the building. Thomas had also acted as treasurer for the project.[9]

A new Church was also proposed for Walton on the Hill, and in 1842 the Salt family gave £200 towards its construction costs of £753. This estimate did not include the tower and the spire, the cost of this was a further £204 12s 0d.

John was not a keen supporter of the railways, being concerned that their building would have a detrimental effect on his estates at Weeping Cross and Standon. It is rather ironic that, despite his opposition to the railway, his body was returned to Stafford by rail following his death in London on 16th August, 1845.

---

[9]Staffordshire Advertiser, 24th July, 1841.

His body was interred in the family vault in the south aisle of St Mary's Church in the presence of his five sons, a grandson and a nephew. The Staffordshire Advertiser states "This town and its institutions have lost a kind, liberal and considerate friend, the Church of England a sincere and conscientious member and one of her warmest supporters, and the great societies connected with her, a generous contributor, who was always ready to further every great work".[10]

John's will was long and complicated, dealing mainly with his estates at Standon and around Eccleshall. One paragraph however, sets out the future of his lands at Weeping Cross.

"I give and devise to my eldest son Thomas, his heirs and assigns for ever leasehold messuages, lands and hereditaments situated at Weeping Cross in the Parish of Berkswich in the County of Stafford and the pews in Baswich Church lately purchased by me together with all my farming live and dead stock, implements of husbandry, household furniture and plate, china, books, wine, linen, garden utensils and other articles and things in upon and about my dwelling houses at Weeping Cross aforesaid. Also I give and devise to my said son Thomas his heirs and assigns the manor or lordship of Standon"[11]

John Stevenson Salt

Just what did Thomas inherit from his father? "The White House", converted from "The Weeping Cross Inn", now comprised a Drawing Room, Dining Room, Study, School Room, Maid's Room, Footman's Room, Butler's Pantry, Kitchen, Scullery, Pantry, Mr Salt's Bedroom and Dressing Room, and the Young Ladies' Room. Outside there was a Dairy, Baking House, Garden House, Hot House, Stable, Slaughter House and two small cottages.

Wheat, turnips, potatoes and barley were growing in the fields and a flock of sheep and 4 milking cows supplied meat and milk for the family!

The estate at Weeping Cross was valued on 28th August 1845 at £728 13 shillings.[12]

---

[10]Staffordshire Advertiser 23rd August, 1845
[11] WSL D1716/5/7
[12] Information from the Inventory & Valuation of Property at Weeping Cross taken for the purpose of proving the will of John Stevenson Salt, in the possession of Sir Michael Salt

Sarah and Harriet Salt

Harriet and Sarah had to share a bedroom in the "White House" and, when young Thomas returned home from boarding school, he would sleep in the second bed in his father's room. The "Spare Room," otherwise known as the "Dressing Room", was stuffed full of furniture, book cases, an easy chair, an assortment of wool and hair mattresses, an iron safe and all sorts of additional clutter!

Now that Thomas was the owner of the property, he decided that it was time to create a much larger and more modern house to accommodate his family and friends.

Chapter 2
Who Built Weeping Cross House?

When was Weeping Cross House built and who was the architect? These are questions that we have asked time and time again without coming up with a definitive answer.

The Chetwynd Pew in Baswich Church restricting the view of the Altar.

Quite by chance a letter found in the Staffordshire County Record Office from Thomas Salt Senior to the Vicar of Berkswich, dated 12th February 1848, gives us a clue. Thomas, as Church Warden at Berkswich, had been trying hard to improve the Church. It would appear that very little maintenance had been carried out since the church had been rebuilt in 1740. Archdeacon Hodson wrote from Lichfield to Thomas in March 1847 saying "I cannot sufficiently express my surprise and regret that so little attention should, in times past, have been paid to the orderly appearance of God's House, and to the comfort of the main body of His worshippers. For while the poorer classes – and I presume, also some of the middle classes – of parishioners have been allowed to sit in seats with cold, damp, bare, stone floors, faculties have been obtained for the erection of gallery-pews, which are not only unsightly in the extreme, but scarcely reverent in their position, and tending to intercept the sight and hearing of the congregation, during those parts of the Service which are read at the Communion Table".[13]

For almost two years Thomas had been trying to persuade the parishioners to agree to improvements and he had made a pledge to the Vicar that he would and

---

[13] SRO D3362/5/43

could resolve the problems. Major Chetwynd at Brocton Hall wanted a Chapel to be built in Brocton, others wanted to extend Walton Church and demolish part of Holy Trinity Church, just leaving a small chapel and the burial ground. The arguments continued until eventually Thomas wrote to the Vicar in desperation saying, "I am now, you are aware, plunged in the trouble and expense of considerable alterations in my house – so I will not pledge myself to do what I promised I would when I hoped the Church question would be settled first".[14]

Weeping Cross 1847

This letter, therefore gives us an approximate date for the building of Weeping Cross House, or as we know it, Baswich House.

Two small paintings on fabric, owned by Sir Michael Salt, seem to confirm that the house was built around this time. One painting shows "The White House" in 1847, the other clearly shows "Weeping Cross House" and is dated 1851.

But there are no clues as to who the architect was. We have looked at Staffordshire architects who could have been responsible. Thomas Trubshaw was the architect of Walton Church but he had died in 1842, and Walton Church was his last. We cannot attribute the House to him. Trubshaw's father James was also an architect but by 1848 he was 71 and we therefore feel it unlikely that he was responsible.

Two other names come to the fore when looking at architects in Stafford around 1840, viz - Joseph Potter and Henry Ward. Joseph Potter was county surveyor for Staffordshire from 1797 until his death in 1842. His death means that he could not have been responsible for Weeping Cross House. However, he did have a son, also called Joseph, who took over his father's architectural business in Lichfield and worked as a church architect. Thomas Salt had dealings with Joseph Potter Junior while sorting out the Baswich Church problems and

Weeping Cross 1851

it is clear that he was not too keen on Mr Potter, who on various occasions had failed to turn up for appointments because he was having problems with his horse! The two men were not on good terms.

---

[14] SRO D3362/5/43

10

To make things doubly complicated, there are two Henry Wards, both architects. We have Henry Ward of Stafford (1806 – 1884) and Henry Ward of Hanley (Born 1801). Time and again we find that Henry Ward of Stafford and Thomas Salt are working together on various projects and we therefore consider that he is the most likely architect for Weeping Cross House. Brancote Farm House, not far from St Thomas' Priory, has a striking resemblance to Weeping Cross House but we have been unable to discover who the architect of this building was.

Brancote Farm

Henry Ward was born in the parish of Castle Church in November 1806. He was apprenticed to Joseph Potter, county surveyor, and in March 1837 Henry married Joseph's daughter Emma. Three months later Emma gave birth to a son, William Wilson Ward. The marriage was short as Emma died in 1844 and only a year later Henry married his second wife Mary Peake.

Henry's first involvement with Thomas Salt seems to occur in 1841 when work commenced on the building of St Paul's Church, Forebridge. Thomas was responsible for fund raising and Henry was appointed architect. These two men are of similar age and Thomas would no doubt feel for Henry when his wife died shortly after the completion of St Paul's Church, leaving him with a young family to raise. Thomas had experienced the same fate when his wife died in 1833 leaving him with three young children.

On 9th May 1845, the spire of Walton Church was struck by lightning and very badly damaged. Thomas Salt was Churchwarden and he called upon Henry Ward to design the new spire. Henry acted as agent for the Churchwardens and employed Samuel Fairhead, Carpenter and Thomas Till, Plumber, to complete the work at a

Walton Church following the lightning strike

cost of £167. Henry was given total control of the project, and it is clear that Thomas Salt had every confidence in him.[15]

Henry continued to design Staffordshire churches. Bednall was built in 1846 and during 1846/47 he worked on the restoration of St John the Baptist Church, Armitage. In 1847 Henry was advertising for builders to work on 5 cottages near

Cottages on Newport Road

---

[15] SRO D3361/5/67

Stafford Station. These cottages are now known as 127 - 133 Newport Road and are listed buildings. Although the scale of these cottages is very different to that of Weeping Cross House there are similarities in the design which can be seen in the windows, the distinctive chimneys and the shape of the doors. He also built the Vicarage at Weston on Trent which is in a very similar style to Weeping Cross House.

By February, 1848 Thomas Salt writes that he is extending his house. We can find no record of Henry Ward working on this building but we are also unable to find any reference to him working on any other buildings in the area at this time. In September 1848 Henry vacated his rented house in Foregate Street[16] and moved to Moss Pit. It would appear that he was now financially sound and his business was doing very well. His new house, although detached, is very similar in style to his cottages on the Newport Road.

Henry was commissioned to work on the restoration of St Chad's Church, Stafford in 1854. Again Thomas Salt was involved in fund raising, and in 1860 Henry was responsible for the design of the new grammar school in Newport Road. We find that Thomas Salt was Chairman of the School Trustees.

Henry Ward's House at Moss Pit

On 12th March 1871, just nine days before his death, Thomas wrote to Hardman & Co. in Birmingham saying "Thank you very much for your last letter. I believe my architect Mr Ward, has sent you zinc patterns of the windows"[17].

---

[16] Staffordshire Advertiser 30th September, 1848
[17] BA Hardman Archive, Letters 1871 "S" Metal

Although the windows he refers to were to be installed in Standon Church, it is clear that the relationship between Salt and Ward continued right up until Thomas' death. Thomas had also ordered new candlesticks and a cross for the Church, and upon his death, his daughter Sarah wrote to Messrs Hardman saying "Will you kindly let me know when the cross and candlesticks my dear father ordered are ready – I imagine you may feel in difficulty what to do with them. Please send them in accordance with his desires and then invoice by post to my brother Thomas Salt Esq. M.P., Weeping Cross, Stafford. We are anxious that my father's wish that they should be presented before Easter Sunday should be fulfilled".[18]

By the 1871 Census, Henry and his family had returned to Stafford town centre, living at 6 Lichfield Street[19], next door to the Sun Inn. Henry and Thomas had worked together over many years. Thomas must have been happy with the standard of workmanship produced by Ward and without more positive evidence we feel that it is more than likely that Ward was responsible for the design of Weeping Cross House.

Later, in 1876, after the death of Thomas Salt Senior, Ward was the architect for Stafford Borough Hall. Henry was also architect for Yarlet Hall, Seighford School and several buildings in Herefordshire.

Ward died at his home in Lichfield Road on 10th August 1884 aged 78.

Stafford Borough Hall

---

[18] BA Hardman Archive, Letters 1871 "S" Metal
[19] Now Lichfield Road

Chapter 3

Schools, Churches and a New House

As a successful banker, Thomas was able to employ staff to keep his home running smoothly. However, life was very different following the death of his wife in 1833. He took solace in his garden winning many prizes at the exhibitions of the Stafford Floral and Horticultural Society, probably with the help of his gardeners. He was also patron of the Stafford Harmonic Society.

Thomas Salt of Weeping Cross 1802 - 1871

As his daughters Harriet and Sarah grew older, he employed Charlotte Huntington, as a governess to take care of their education.[20] Young Thomas, however, was sent away to school. Because he was far too young to go to Rugby School as his father had always intended, he was dispatched to Mr Rawson's School in Seaforth, close to the mouth of the River Mersey.

In 1813 John Gladstone, father of William Gladstone, a merchant, shipbuilder and slave owner with sugar plantations in Demerara, bought 100 acres of Litherland Marsh on which he built Seaforth House. Litherland was then a very pretty coastal village. In 1814, after he was elected M.P. for Liverpool, Gladstone set about building a new church for the area and, once the church was complete, he invited William Rawson of Cheshire to become vicar and start a small boarding school for his own four sons and other well-to-do boys from the North West, preparing them for admission to public schools. This was the school where Thomas was to go as a young boy.

Eventually, in February 1844 just before his fourteenth birthday Thomas left Mr Rawson's school and entered Rugby. Here he was to remain until 1849, gaining, while in the sixth form, the English Essay prize. He was then accepted at Balliol College, Oxford, where he studied Law and History, gaining a First Class Honours degree in 1853. As was, and still is, the practice at Oxford, seven years after graduation a BA degree can be converted, without further study or residence, into an

---

[20] 1841 Census

M.A. So, in due course, Thomas Salt, by payment of a small sum,[21] was able to add the letters M.A. after his name.

In the 1830's there was a national move to build schools for the "working classes". The Earl of Lichfield donated a piece of land at Walton and, in April 1836, the great and the good of the area contributed towards a building fund for a village school. John Stevenson Salt and his wife headed the list of subscriptions, followed by his sons Thomas, William and John, together with a contribution of £15 from his daughters. Thomas, as Church Warden, was involved, at every stage, with the construction of the school and the appointment of staff. At a meeting held at Milford Hall on 29th November, 1836 Thomas was appointed treasurer and all subscriptions had to be paid into his bank. He was keen to see that all children had the opportunity of a basic education, although it was not always appreciated by parents when children were taken away from working in the fields, especially at harvest time.

Walton School built 1838

The financial state of Stafford Borough was in rather a mess in the 1840's and 1850's and Thomas Salt came to the town's aid. The Mayor and Aldermen had found it necessary to borrow £7000 and then another £1000 from Thomas Salt's Bank. When the time came to repay the money the town worthies declared that they were "not provided with sufficient monies"[22]. An application was then made to the Lords Commissioners of her Majesty's Treasury for a loan of £11,000 on security of the whole of their corporate property. This included much of the centre of Stafford, namely North and South Backwalls, Eastgate, Foregate, Tenterbanks, Broad Eye and much more.

Such was the anger of Stafford residents at this proposal to mortgage more of the towns assets that, following a well attended public meeting, they also wrote to the Treasury "Praying their Lordships to withhold their sanction to the sale of any further property belonging to the burgesses of this Borough without diligent and searching inquiry being first instigated into the expenditure". Over 850 Burgesses of Stafford signed this petition.

The Mayor and Aldermen came up with an explanation for the Treasury and, eventually, the Salt bank was repaid with interest.

Thomas Salt Senior had been involved with the restoration of St Mary's Church, working with George Gilbert Scott. Then, in 1854 Thomas worked with the architect Henry Ward in the restoration of St Chad's Church, which was in a very poor state of repair. Under the guidance of Thomas, funds were raised to restore the

---

[21] In 2009 the fee to gain an MA degree is £20
[22] SRO D1323/0/2/1/14-15

chancel in memory of Isaac Walton who, although he had been born just a stone's throw away from the church, had, at that time, no permanent memorial in the town. The plaster, which had covered much of the interior of the church for two hundred years, was removed from the chancel arch revealing the fine 12th century stone carvings we know today. Windows were altered or removed and restored, but at this time funds did not permit the complete restoration of the church.

St Chad's Church by J.L. Petit

In 1848 Thomas had commenced his expensive building programme for his new house. It was however, over ten years before Weeping Cross House and grounds were eventually opened for all to see. On Whit Tuesday, the 14th June, 1859, he held a Grand Rural Fête. This report appeared in the Staffordshire Advertiser the following week:

"Tuesday last will be long remembered by hundreds in this town as the day on which the delightful grounds and gardens at Weeping Cross, belonging to Thomas Salt, Esq., were first thrown open to the public. The weather was lovely - all that could be wished for by those who desired a day's enjoyment and recreation; and taking advantage of it, the road from Stafford to Weeping Cross for several hours presented a continuous stream of living beings. At one o'clock the tradesmen closed their shops and business was suspended. A few hours later in the day a stranger would have imagined the town had been deserted for it was only now and then that a human creature could be seen in the streets, or that a sound broke in on the quietude which reigned around.

This partial emptying of the town, however, brought together several thousand persons in the grounds at Weeping Cross, where the committee of the Mechanics'

Institution[23] (for the benefit of the funds of which the fête was held) had provided a large store of enjoyment, suitable for all classes and all ages. Large tents had been erected for the sale of refreshments, which were well supplied by Mr Ball and Mr Heath: and the copious draughts offered to Bacchus made many of his votaries[24] "more merry than wise". Confectionery and other stalls were also numerous, and received their due share of support.

Weeping Cross House, showing the bowling green

The amusements commenced with a foot race, at two o'clock, which was followed by a hurdle race, for which prizes were given. There was also a "stag hunt": and at five o'clock five members of the institution contended, in a quarter of a mile race, for a large edition of Shakspere[(sic)]. The prize was, after a well-contested race, won by Mr George Collier. Old English games were numerous, but the most exciting and laughable of the entertainments was the unpacking of a lottery box. The box was suspended midway on a high pole, and as each successive adventurer climbed the pole, and explored the various departments within, he was met with clouds of coloured dust, which quickly descended on the crowds of anxious gazers, whose hurried flight and sorry appearance caused the greatest amusement to those whom distance rendered more fortunate.

At four o'clock an open-air concert took place, the performers, upwards of 30, being chiefly members of the institution. The pieces selected were of a miscellaneous character, and the performers, both vocal and instrumental, acquitted themselves well. If the chorus had numbered 300 instead of 30 voices the concert would have caused a very pleasing effect; but, as it was, they could be heard only a short distance beyond the platform on which they were ranged.

---

[23] Information regarding the Mechanics Institute can be found later in the chapter.
[24] Votaries. One who is devoted or passionately addicted to some particular pursuit or occupation.

On the green close to the house, several gentlemen were engaged in the scientific game of bowls, others joined in the more athletic game of quoits, and not a few practised themselves in archery. But, as is usual on all such occasions, the all absorbing recreation was dancing, and in this exercise the fair sex especially were most enthusiastic. The fine band of the Queen's Own Royal Staffordshire Yeomanry, under the leadership of Mr Onions, and the Stafford Juvenile Flute and Drum Band, both attired in uniform, lent most effective aid to the dancers, and so greatly did hundreds of those present enjoy this exciting pastime, that the shades of night alone seemed to check what youth and energy would fain have prolonged to a more advanced hour. The entertainments were brought to a close by a very beautiful display of fireworks, by Mr William Bibby, of Birmingham: and we must not forget to mention that several very large balloons were sent up during the day in most excellent style by William Taylor of this town.

Lyceum Theatre, Martin Street

The worthy owner of the Estate, Thomas Salt, Esq., invited several of his personal friends and many other respectable persons to partake of refreshments in the dining-room, where a cold collation, with a profusion of wines, fruits etc was placed before his guests. Captain Salt, M.P., with other members of the family, were also present during the day, and it must have afforded them the most heartfelt satisfaction to witness the hundreds whom their kindness had on that day rendered happy and joyful, whilst many of the gallant member's more zealous partisans strove with each other in expressing their joyous enthusiasm at meeting him. We understand that the fête has been one of the most successful held in the neighbourhood, and that the committee will be able to place a balance of nearly £80 to the funds of the institution."

The Mechanic's Institute, was established as an "aid for cultivating and exercising the mental powers" of its members as well as being concerned with their moral and intellectual advancement. It was situated at the rear of the Lyceum Theatre in Martin Street and possessed a large Reading Room which was open from 9 a.m. until 10 p.m. As well as a library of over 3,000 books, it contained newspapers, periodicals and reference books. Lectures and entertainments were given during the year, and members were able to obtain tickets at half-price on production of their membership card.[25]

---

[25] The Mechanics Institute Library was dispersed in1894 following the establishment of the Free Library.

Thomas Junior had been elected to Parliament just a few weeks earlier and the Grand Fête was perhaps the first opportunity he had to mingle with the people of Stafford and with the influential members of the community who had supported him.

Emma Helen Mary Anderdon in 1861

In 1861 he married Emma Helen Mary, (known as Helen) youngest daughter of John Lavincount Anderdon, at the Old Parish Church, Chislehurst. Helen's father was a writer on angling and devotional subjects and, in 1845, he published "The River Dove: with some Quiet Thoughts on the Happy Practise of Angling", dedicated to Isaac Walton and Charles Cotton. Helen's mother, Anna Maria, was the daughter of William Manning M.P. and her uncle was Cardinal Manning, a Roman Catholic convert who would become Cardinal Archbishop of Westminster. Although the newly weds spent much of their time in London, they were able to lease a house in Walton-on-the-Hill from the Earl of Lichfield. This was their Staffordshire home until 1871 when Thomas Junior inherited Weeping Cross House.[26]

By 1870 Thomas Salt senior's health was failing. He was confined to bed and his daughter Sarah was on hand to make his life as comfortable as possible. Sarah would take down letters that Thomas dictated and then they would be signed in a very frail, shaky hand. It was clear that there was nothing wrong with Thomas' mind and he continued to act as Churchwarden of Baswich. On 20th December, 1870 (Tuesday) Thomas wrote to Messrs. Hardman of New Hall Hill, Birmingham, saying "I am very unwell and cannot manage it myself. Will you kindly get me, from a good maker, four bell ropes of the enclosed length and strength at your earliest convenience, or send this letter to them. Must have them by Friday."[27] Thomas did receive his bell ropes by Friday and they were fitted to the bells in Baswich Church in time for Christmas. If only we received such service today!

Thomas died on 21st March, 1871. In accordance with his wishes, the funeral took place at sunset at Baswich Church. His body was carried from Weeping Cross to the church by twelve of the oldest labourers from the estate, some of whom were very old indeed. He was buried in a plain grave near to that of his grand-daughter, Violet Blanche, the daughter of Thomas Salt, junior, who had died, aged just seven

---

[25] It has always been presumed that the family spent their married life when not in London, at Weeping Cross. It is only while researching this book that we have discovered that they lived in Walton on the Hill following their marriage until Thomas Salt senior died in 1871.
[27] BA Hardman Archives Letters 1870 "S" Metal

months, in 1868. "At the conclusion of the burial service the choir sang "Abide with me", from Hymns Ancient & Modern, Thus ended a simple but solemn ceremony which will be long remembered by all who witnessed it. The residents of the neighbourhood showed their respect for the deceased gentleman's memory by drawing their blinds. At Stafford the tradesmen partially closed their shops and the bells of St Mary's Church rang muffled peals on Saturday afternoon and Sunday. The Rev H.A. Fuller at Baswich Church on Sunday and at Walton in the afternoon feelingly alluded in his sermon to the great loss that the parish had sustained but forbore to dwell at any length on Mr Salt's virtues, rightly considering that nothing would have been more out of keeping with that great humility which was one of their departed friend's leading traits."[28]

The Weeping Cross Estate was left to his son Thomas. Daughters Sarah and Harriet each received £500 per year for life.   This equates to around £50,000 p.a. today.

Following Thomas' death, it was decided that the nave of St Chad's Church should be restored in his memory. George Gilbert Scott drew up the plans and, although the work started in 1874, it was not until the 1880's that the restoration was eventually finished. George Gilbert Scott died in 1878 and did not see his work completed.

If you visit St Chad's Church today you will find, just inside the west door, a plaque to the memory of Thomas Salt, Senior. It says "To the Glory of God and in memory of Thomas Salt of Weeping Cross, Esquire constant promoter of every good work in this town and County. The nave of this church was restored to its original solemnity and beauty by many friends and neighbours. AD 1874."

St Chad's Church during restoration

[28] Staffordshire Advertiser 1st April, 1871

Chapter 4
Thomas Salt, Member of Parliament

Thomas Salt Junior, often known as Captain Salt, to distinguish him from his father, had a first class brain; he required more than just a job in a bank. He had a desire to become a Member of Parliament and so decided to stand at the election in May 1859 when he was just twenty-nine. Procedures then for electing an M.P. were very different from the way things are done today! Only adult males owning or occupying property worth at least £10 per annum, provided that they had been in possession of the property for at least one year and had paid all contingent taxes arising from the property, and who had not received any parochial poor relief in the previous year, were eligible to vote.

At 10 o'clock on 30th April 1859 the Mayor walked from the Guildhall into the Market Square where five wagons had been arranged in a semi-circle. Stafford was to send two Members of Parliament to London and four candidates had put themselves forward for the honour of representing the town. Mr Wise, the sitting M.P. was not present but on the wagons stood Alderman Sidney on the right, Captain Thomas Salt on the left and on the extreme left was Colonel Addison with his rather noisy friends. The Mayor stood on the central wagon.

Market Square, 1859

Captain Salt was proposed by Alderman Morgan, who said that "here was a young man who appeared for the first time against three old electioneerers. He had known Captain Salt since childhood, whose family had been burgesses for the last three generations, and whose name was associated with all that was good and commendable in the borough. He therefore proposed Thomas Salt as a proper person to become one of our representatives in Parliament."

Thomas was then given the opportunity to address the crowd but his speech was shortened, and almost drowned out by a torrential rain storm. Throughout his life Thomas was described as being quiet and gentle and his speech indicated that he did not enjoy the noise and clamour of a great mass of people. He said, "I would rather satisfy you by talking about politics with you at your homes than on a platform, and wish to be judged by deeds rather than by words."

As the rain eased a little, the Mayor asked for a show of hands in favour of Mr Wise. Nearly all of the 2000 people present held up their hands. About 350 hands were displayed for Alderman Sidney, a large number supported Captain Salt and about three-quarters of those present supported Colonel Addison. The Mayor indicated that, on a show of hands Wise and Addison had received the most votes and were considered elected. However, a poll was demanded on behalf of Thomas Salt and Alderman Sidney. This would take place the following Saturday. Names of those people eligible to vote were entered into a Poll Book and as each person cast their vote, a record of their chosen candidate was marked against their name. As the day progressed, a total of votes cast so far was available for all to see. At 10 a.m. the voting was as follows:-

Wise - 527, Salt - 302, Sidney - 241, Addison - 118

At noon Wise and Salt were well in the lead and by 4 p.m. when voting closed, the final result was Wise - 911, Salt - 624, Sidney - 366, Addison -181.

The newly elected young Conservative M.P. attempted to address the crowd gathered in the Market Place, but for several minutes the meeting kept up a continuous roar of groans and hisses and not one word could be heard. Thomas gave up and left for home. He would be heard on another day in another place. His celebration dinner was held at the Maid's Head Inn towards the end of May where, after a first rate meal, a large number of toasts were proposed, some excellent songs were sung, and a most convivial evening was had by all.

The Maid's Head Inn, Gaolgate, Stafford

Thomas did not stand at the Elections of 1865 and 1868 as his business commitments, the death of his baby daughter Violet, and his rapidly growing family prevented him spending much time in London. However, the election results for 1868 were contested. Not everyone was happy with the result and with the behaviour of the supporters of the elected candidates.

After an investigation lasting 9 days, Mr Justice Blackburn decided that the election for Stafford was void in the case of both members. (Henry Pochin and Walter Meller). There were charges of "treating" and "bribery", and witnesses gave evidence of being offered amounts of up to £10, a considerable sum in 1859, to vote for the Liberals. Following the publication of Mr Justice Blackburn's findings, a by-election was called for early in 1869. Thomas Salt once again put himself forward. At 4.30 p.m. on Polling Day 3,000 people filled the Market Square awaiting the declaration of the results. Many of them were drunk, and the police were needed to calm things down when one "gentleman" tried to drive his butcher's cart at full pelt through the crowd! Thomas Salt and Captain Talbot were duly elected.

It was during this Parliament that Thomas introduced the Private Chapels Act, which became known as "Salt's Act". This Act gave power to the Bishops to licence a clergyman to conduct services in private chapels of a certain character, such as chapels in hospitals, colleges or similar institutions without requiring the approval of the incumbent of the parish. Throughout his Parliamentary career Thomas took special interest in matters relating to the Established Church of England and to education.

By 1874 secret voting had been introduced, and the fight for the Stafford seats was hard, with many political meetings being held throughout the town. Salt was elected again along with Alexander Macdonald, a result which caused much comment in the national press. One paper reported "Stafford has won for itself the great distinction of being the first constituency to return a genuine working man to Parliament. Alexander Macdonald is a representative of the miners being the secretary of one of the largest associations of that class of artisan". During this Parliament Thomas was appointed Parliamentary Secretary to the Local Government Board.

In 1880 Thomas stood once again, this time against Alexander Macdonald and an up-and-coming young Barrister, Charles Benjamin Bright McLaren from Edinburgh. In 1877 McLaren had married Laura Pochin, daughter of Henry Pochin, the Stafford M.P. who had been unseated in 1869. At a public meeting in support of Salt the Chairman said of McLaren, "If Mr McLaren were not good enough to put up for a

Swan Hotel

constituency in his own country why should he come and try to palm himself off on the ancient borough of Stafford!

Voting commenced at eight o'clock and before long the town was invaded by groups of young men and boys all wearing green favours, the colour of the Liberal party. Anyone displaying the blue of the Conservatives was likely to be roughly handled. Thomas and his Conservative colleague, Gerald F. Talbot, were pelted with mud while driving through Broad Eye and Thomas suffered a cut hand from a flying stone. After the close of the polls at four o'clock there was a mêlée in the street outside The Swan, headquarters of the Conservatives. In an attempt to cool tempers one well meaning servant threw cold water on the crowd from an upper window. This did not have the desired effect. Stones were thrown and considerable damage was done to the front windows of the hotel. The police were soon on the spot and remained on duty for the rest of the evening in order to protect the Swan and its guests.

The Liberals were to win both seats, with McLaren topping the poll, followed by Alexander Macdonald. Thomas Salt and Gerald Talbot received the news at the Swan at around seven thirty. Before returning home to Weeping Cross the defeated M.P. stated that he was ready at any future time to come forward and fight the battle for the Conservatives at Stafford. It was not until 10 o'clock that the crowd had dispersed from outside the Swan. Seventy police officers from Stafford and Stone had been present in the town that day to prevent any disturbance getting out of hand.

Thomas would be back in Parliament before long! Alexander Macdonald had not been in good health at the time of the election and by the end of October 1881 he was dead. The by-election was held on 19th November, a Saturday, causing great dissatisfaction amongst the tradesmen of the town as they felt they would lose business. This time the fight was between Thomas Salt and Liberal candidate, George Howell. The Mayor appealed to the inhabitants of the town, regardless of their political persuasion, to keep calm and not provoke any disturbance. He made it clear that the Police had strict orders to arrest any person committing a breach of the peace!

The day went off without undue trouble; the only crime appeared to be the theft of a 25 guinea watch from Mr Harris, a shoe manufacturer. Counting, at the Guildhall, commenced at quarter to five and the result was declared from the balcony at 6.20 p.m. Thomas Salt was once again an M.P. for Stafford, polling 297 votes more than his rival.

By the next general election in November 1885, the rules had changed and Stafford was to return only one M.P. instead of two.

Charles Benjamin Bright McLaren
Later 1st Baron Aberconway

ELECTORS OF STAFFORD.

Why is Mr. Salt afraid of answering questions at Public Meetings ?

Is he afraid of having to confess that, although a professed friend of Religion and Morality, he absented himself from every division on the Criminal Amendment Bill for the Protection of Young Girls ?

Is he afraid of having to confess that, although a professed friend of the Poor, he never voted for the Poor having a vote; but out of the 25 divisions on the Franchise Bill, he 10 times voted against it, and 15 times absented himself ?

Is he afraid of having to confess that he voted in favour of reducing the County Rates and Taxes on Land at the expense of the Taxpayers in Towns ?

Is he afraid of having to confess that, although he professes not to be a party man, he was one of the seven gentlemen in whose hands were placed £70,000 to help the Tory Party at the last General Election in 1880 (see "Times," April 17th, 1884), and that he never gave a Liberal Vote in his life ?

Is he afraid of having to confess that he voted for the abominable Tory Slave Circular that took away the protection of the British Flag from the poor fugitive Slave ?

Is he afraid of having to confess that he voted in favour of Flogging our Soldiers and Sailors ?

Is he afraid of having to confess that he has always voted for the rich against the poor, and for the strong against the weak ?

Is he afraid of having to confess that when the Tories in the House of Commons tried to take away the contract for Engines, which Mr. Gladstone's Government gave to Stafford, he absented himself from the House, and left Mr. McLaren to defend the town and trade of Stafford ?

Is he afraid of having to confess that he never gave a single vote in Parliament for the benefit of the town of Stafford, but, on the contrary, was a member of the Tory Government which, by passing the Prisons Bill, took away a great deal of trade from the town ?

Is he afraid of having to confess that he wants to go to Parliament to follow a leader whom two or three weeks ago he called a "Political Mountebank" ?

ANTI-HUMBUG.

Printed and Published by Drewry & Whitaker, Eastgate Street, Stafford.

Liberal Poster for the 1885 Election

It was at this election that the ladies began to take an active interest in events, filling the gallery at a public meeting at the Borough Hall in support of Thomas Salt. Polling took place on Wednesday and most of the Shoe Factories in the town were closed throughout the day. During the afternoon many of the shops put up their shutters for safety's sake. The town was the scene of great excitement. Fights between rival factions were common place, keeping the 100 police officers on duty in the town fully occupied! The polling stations were open for twelve hours, from 8 am – 8 p.m. and the count was completed just before 10 p.m. Thomas was to lose his seat to McLaren by just 47 votes, but he vowed to fight on at the next election.

Following his defeat Thomas published a poster thanking his supporters, in which he said "I can look back with satisfaction to many long years of hard work as your representative in Parliament; and this position has led to much happy intercourse with persons of every rank, in respect of your social, domestic, and local affairs. It is, perhaps not unnatural that you should have grown tired of me, and that you prefer the voice and the words of a stranger. But I again warn you that empty promises, violent changes, unfounded expectation, will bring misfortune instead of happiness to the poor man. I am grateful to my friends for many acts of kindness, which will ever last in my memory. And now I heartily bid you farewell". In response the Liberals penned and published this poem!

PARODY ON THE HEARTY "FAREWELL"

Now Stafford men, I wish you all a very long "Farewell"
My Heart is broken and my grief all words will fail to tell
You knew my Pa, you knew my Ma, you know well what I am
Yet you've given the cold shoulder to the poor neglected lamb.
CHORUS (*Pensively*) –   *O Stafford, dear Stafford,*
                            Plainly do I see,
                            The Liberal Mac is on your back
                            And leaves no room for me.

Your reason for deserting me I cannot understand;
As a neighbour I am perfect, as any in the land,
Because my politics don't suit, the Town must suffer loss,
Instead of going to Parliament I'm off to Weeping Cross.
CHORUS – *O Stafford, dear Stafford etc.*

You've left your lover in the lurch, and took the other man –
Now after this desertion, you must do the best you can;-
Weeping Cross will be "To Let", for ever and for aye;
And you'll cry in vain for Salt and Soup to cheer you on your way
CHORUS – *O Stafford, dear Stafford etc.*

I'm not surprised you're tired of me-your love has now grown cold:
Politics are not my "fort", I've frequently been told;
But still I thought, for mother's sake, and for my father's too,
That Stafford men would ne'er forsake the wearing of the blue.
CHORUS – *O Stafford, dear Stafford etc*

The "tie" which has united us is broken once again;
"Tis not my choice, but yours" which fills my heart with grief and pain;-
And after all I've done for you, it's hard to get the sack,
So now I really mean "Farewell" and never shall come back.
> CHORUS – *O Stafford, mad Stafford,*
> *This action you will rue:*
> *"Farewell" again, I say "Farewell",*
> *For Salt has done with you.*[29]

Within seven months another general election had been called. This time McLaren was defeated by 93 votes!

Pressure of work, both in Parliament and at the Bank (he had been Chairman of Lloyds Bank since 1886), had taken its toll on Thomas' health, and when the election was called in 1892 Thomas, at the age of 62, decided it was time to retire. In a poster addressed to the burgesses and electors of the Borough of Stafford Thomas said "It is a matter of almost equal disappointment to me that I am compelled to seek immediate rest and change, and am therefore unable to assist even in a small degree by my voice and my presence at a most important political contest". Mr Douglas Straight fought the seat, unsuccessfully, for the Conservatives.

Thomas and his wife spent some time travelling all around the world and eventually returned to the U.K. in exceedingly good health. Thomas was persuaded to stand for the Conservatives again at the 1895 election. He admitted that he felt twenty years younger than he had in 1892 and promised that he would do everything he could to regain the seat. His supporters hoped that he would, if elected achieve a Cabinet post. On Polling Day the Conservatives wore a blue cornflower tied with blue ribbon in their lapels while the Liberals sported the usual green and pink ribbons. Once again the shops and factories were closed. When the count had been completed only twelve votes separated the two candidates. Mr Salt did not address his supporters but bore his defeat philosophically, retiring to his home at Weeping Cross as early as possible. It was the end of Thomas Salt's political career.

---

[29] SRO D256/29/13/2

Chapter 5
The Salt Family and King Edward VI Grammar School

For many years the Salts, both father and son, were involved with Stafford's King Edward VI Grammar School and the building on Newport Road was constructed with considerable financial support from the family.

"King Edward VI, by letters patent on 10th December, 1551, on the petition of the inhabitants and burgesses of the town of Stafford, granted and ordained that there should be one Grammar School in Stafford. To be called the Free Grammar School of King Edward VI, for the education of boys and youths in grammar, and one schoolmaster and one usher, to continue forever."

The School started its life in St Bertelin's Chapel, adjoining St Mary's Church and here it remained for over two hundred years. In 1813 it moved to new premises in Gaol Square. The building stood in a small yard over a former stable that contained the privies, coal, and dust bins. It consisted of a single room divided into two "schools", English and Latin. At one end was a series of pigeon holes for storing books and outdoor clothes. The nine sash windows were often broken by boys throwing stones from the street. It was demolished in the 1970's when Gaol Square was developed.

The "Old" Grammar School, North Walls

Thomas Salt Senior was concerned about the state of the school and, as Chairman of the Trustees he wrote to the Press, in December 1857, explaining how bad things had been. "Previously to the year 1843, we were much disturbed to find the School sadly neglected, and almost entirely unattended: indeed, I believe at one time, there were two paid Masters and only *one* boy".

Despite the efforts of the Trustees to improve things, by 1860 the school was described in the following terms. "Of all the dirty, filthy places I have ever visited, that was the dirtiest. The desks were covered with dust, and the water closets were in a most filthy state. This was not surprising since the only cleaners were four boys who were the recipients of Sutton's charity."

By 1930 Daniel Grattidge was the only surviving person who had attended the school when it was in North Walls, and he remembers that there was an annual feast. He also says that money was allowed for fireworks on 5th November.

The Old Grammar School, North Walls

This allowance was stopped owing to an accident (Health & Safety even in the 1850's) whereupon the boys formed a deputation, and went to see Mr Salt, Chairman of the Trustees, at his house at Weeping Cross. He received them very hospitably, but could not permit the allowance for fireworks to continue; however he gave the boys some for themselves."[30]

The school and its charities should have been run by 17 Trustees but this was not the case. Of the 17 persons appointed 8 were dead, 3 were non-resident in Stafford, leaving just 6 to act as Trustees. These 6 were the Mayor, John Griffin,

---

[30] WSL. Notes for a history of King Edward VI School.

Thomas Salt Senior, Dr Edward Knight, James Turnock, gentleman, Edward Lloyd, manufacturer and the Rector of Tixall, Rev. William Webb. An application was made to the Master of the Rolls for permission to remove the 3 non-resident trustees and to include other upstanding members of Stafford society including Thomas Salt M.P. (son of the Chairman), Robert Hand (solicitor and Town Clerk since 1858), who would build a house opposite the Chairman at Weeping Cross, and John Webb, Banker in the Chairman's Bank.

Following petitions and counter petitions, a new scheme was drawn up in 22nd June, 1858, and new laws were added allowing for 17 Trustees of the Church of England. The Trustees were no longer appointed for life. They were now able to resign their office by giving the required notice, or upon leaving the established church, or by an absence of 2 years from Trustee meetings.

Having resolved the problems of the Trustees, it was necessary to make a fresh start with a new headmaster. The Trustees decided that the Rev George Norman should be relieved of his duties and given a pension of £35. The original proposal was for a pension of £50 a year but this was reduced after protests. The offer of a pension to someone who was considered to have been negligent in performing his duties did not meet with the approval of everyone! This resulted in an inquiry where there was much discussion, arguments and calling of witnesses. William Whale, aged twelve, said he "had been in the Grammar School nearly two years; he left at Christmas, 1858. During that time the head master was in the habit of arriving between eleven and twelve, and left between three and four, except on Friday, when he stayed an hour longer to hear the Catechism. Mr. Norman frequently sent him, and other boys, out for wine; the bottle was covered over with paper. Mr. Norman used often to sit drinking at his desk, but he had never seen him intoxicated". Despite such testimony against him, Rev Norman was eventually allocated his £35 per annum pension.

On 16th January, 1860 the Rev. Frederick Clark, M.A. of Clare College, Cambridge was appointed Headmaster.   Two months later, on 6th March, a Public Meeting was held to discuss the erection of a new Grammar School and Master's House. At this meeting there was some dissent, it being suggested that there was some shady dealing between Mr Webb and the other trustees over the exchange of land. Thomas Salt and Webb were both directors of Stevenson, Salt and Webb Bank. One resident said all that was needed was a new Headmaster, the present school being good enough and large enough for the purpose for which it was required and which, with a small outlay, it might be made very comfortable. This objector failed to take into account "the foul smelling brook running close to the school" which was one of the main reasons a new site was preferred.

Eventually an inquiry was ordered by the Charity Commissioners and carried out by Mr F.O. Martin. He was of the opinion that the premises in Gaol Square were no longer "fit for purpose" and that a new school was needed as soon as possible. The provision of a Master's House on the premises would allow for a few boarders, and their fees would help keep the school running while cash was tight. The new school cost £3,258 to build, much more than the original budget. Money was raised by the sale of land to the Railway Company, the sale of the old school, and a loan of £500 from Thomas Salt.

As the new school neared completion, the "Staffordshire Advertiser" carried the following report. "The new erection is divided into two chambers, for the upper and lower school respectively, each apartment being 60 or 70 feet long by 30 feet wide. The school has an open timber roof of considerable altitude, which affords ample open ventilation, and its large windows give an abundance of light. Added to this it will accommodate 104 scholars – a much greater number than could formerly be taught. The master's house adjoining, which stands upon a somewhat larger area of ground, contains several classrooms for tuition in special subjects such as modern languages. On its top storey are arranged the sleeping rooms for the private boarders, which have a direct communication with the school by means of a staircase winding within a small bell turret at the side of the building. Its cost is about £3,000. Mr Ward is the architect and Mr Espley the builder.

After leaving the splendid structure recently erected as a railway station, the stranger must consider it worthy of its position as the first object of attention in Stafford. Under the management of the Rev. F.K. Clarke, the number of scholars has been gradually increasing, and what is more important, the standard of acquirement has been raised.

We cannot conclude this brief notice without mentioning that a gentleman of the town has exhibited his warm interest in the school by having constructed at considerable expense, an excellent fives court in the playground."[31]

The original £3,000 costs did not make allowance for building the cloisters and chapel. The further £250 required was raised by subscription. Over half of this amount was donated by the Salt family.

The Grammar School seen from the rear.

The new school continued to thrive with the support of the Trustees, including Thomas Salt Senior, his son, and its new headmaster. Thomas, junior, was appointed a school governor in 1873, when a new scheme was introduced

---

[31] Staffordshire Advertiser 10th May 1862

throughout the country. He continued in this post until his death, always taking a great interest in the school.

In 1883, Mrs Salt presented the school with a sports trophy - the Mile Challenge Cup. This was competed for on an annual basis until it was won in three successive years (1917, 1918 & 1919) by Eric Ward, who was awarded the trophy outright.

A new headmaster, Mr E.A. Powell, arrived in 1901. Just three years later Thomas Salt Junior, now Sir Thomas, and still a great friend of the school died. To mark the support he had given to the school for over forty years, it was decided to extend the buildings in his memory. By enlarging the school it would qualify as a secondary school and the Board of Education would provide grants of £200 a year.

A request for donations towards this memorial failed to cover the estimated cost of building and so, on 25th and 26h July, 1906, a Grand Fête was held at the school. The aim was to raise £500 towards providing a miniature Rifle Range (strongly advocated by Earl Roberts, KG) a covered Drill Ground so that physical exercise could take place whatever the weather, and a bicycle shed.

The Grammar School circa 1908 following the building of the extension in memory of Sir Thomas Salt

The centre of Stafford was decorated with flags and bunting on the days of the Fête. There was to be no excuse for residents being unaware of the event. On Tuesday 25th the Dowager Countess of Shrewsbury opened proceedings in the presence of Lady Helen Salt, who was accompanied by her son and daughter-in-law. The Earl of Shrewsbury was unable to attend as he was in Llandrindod Wells attempting to get rid of an attack of gout! The grounds of the school were covered in tents and marquees and the Headmasters room was turned into a bar for two days.

On the following day, Mrs T.S. Twyford, wife of the High Sheriff of the County arrived in the State Carriage to declare the Fête open! At the end of it all the grand sum of £600 had been raised and the extensions to the school, in memory of Sir Thomas Salt, went ahead.

The High Sheriff's State Carriage photographed in 1909

Chapter 6
A New Library

The Salt family made their money from banking. The name of the family banks changed several times over the years from Stevenson Salt & Co, based in the Stafford Old Bank, to Bosanquet, Salt & Co in Lombard Street, London. In 1847 the London Gazette shows that the Stevenson, Salt & Sons bank at 20 Lombard Street was being run by three of John Stevenson Salt's sons; John (1806-1856), William (1801-1863) and George (1820-1858). The eldest son, Thomas (1802-1871) was running the Stafford. Bank in the Market Square.

After mergers the name changed to Lloyds, Barnetts & Bosanquet Bank Ltd with the head office in Birmingham. This was soon simplified to Lloyds Bank Ltd. Thomas Salt Junior had been a director for a number of years and he eventually became Chairman of Lloyds in 1886, a post he would hold until 1898. Thomas was also President of the Institute of Bankers from 1891 to 1893.

Stafford Old Bank

We will not dwell on the family's banking history as it has been well documented in other books. Our interest is in William who, after almost 150 years, continues to have an influence on the work of Staffordshire historians today.

William was the third son of John Stevenson Salt and Sarah Stevenson, and was born at 9, Russell Square, London on 29th October, 1808. He spent his whole life living in London and working in the Bank. However, his great passion was for collecting books, manuscripts, maps and paintings - in fact anything to do with the history of Staffordshire. He commissioned such artists as Thomas Peploe Wood and John Buckler to paint local views and gradually, with the financial security which the bank allowed, he created an extensive archive covering all aspects of life in the County.

William married Helen Black on the 29th October 1857, his 49th birthday. The couple had been neighbours in Russell Square, and William's younger sister Harriett had married Helen's brother, Alexander, six years earlier. The marriage was short. William collapsed at church on 6th December 1863. He was taken home in a cab but died within half an hour of returning at the age of fifty-five.

Standon Church by Thomas Peploe Wood

Helen became the keeper of William's collection which must have taken up a considerable amount of room in their home. In 1865 she offered the collection to Lichfield Cathedral Library but, after lengthy negotiations, the Cathedral refused to comply with the conditions Mrs Salt was imposing on them. Eventually, in 1868, Helen declared that the collection had to go. She approached Sotheby's who prepared a catalogue ready to sell everything at an auction which was expected to last twelve days. The coins and medals were sold on 21st April, 1868.

Before the auction of the remainder of the collection could take place, someone contacted Mrs Salt and the sale was cancelled. It is not known who made the approach; perhaps it was William's older brother Thomas, as he was living in Staffordshire and no doubt appreciated the importance of the collection to the county. Or maybe it was the Earl of Lichfield for, by the autumn of 1868, the collection had been sent to Shugborough for safe keeping. It remained there for four years.

It was now necessary to make some decisions as to the future of the collection. Mrs Salt requested that an endowment fund be set up and she asked that £10,000 be raised before she would finally hand over ownership. Meetings were held to try and raise the necessary funds but only £1,700 was forthcoming. The Bodleian Library at Oxford now offered to take care of the collection. To prevent the archives going out of Staffordshire the Earl of Lichfield exerted his powers of persuasion and Mrs Salt eventually agreed to reduce the endowment to £6,000 but gave the county just three months to find the money. Otherwise it would go elsewhere.

Thomas Salt Junior, anxious that his uncle's collection should remain in Staffordshire, offered a house in Market Square for use as a Library and other purposes. Mrs Salt did not like this idea, wanting the building to be used entirely for the collection. She withdrew her offer intending to sell everything to the Bodleian. Eventually she came back with one final offer. She would buy the house in Market Square from her nephew to be used to house the collection. However, the County must still raise £6,000 within three months. Thomas sold the house to his aunt and then donated £2,000 (the price his aunt had paid for the house) toward the final £6,000 total. The deadline for raising the money was 30th March, 1872. The target was reached just in time and, thanks mainly to the tremendous generosity of Thomas Salt Junior, of Weeping Cross House, we now have a fantastic library of which the County should be proud.

It was a difficult and time consuming process to catalogue William's collection, and it was not until January 1874 that the William Salt Library eventually opened its doors. The first visitor was the Mayor of Stafford, Mr John Kelsall.[32]

Such was the extent of the collection, there was never sufficient room in the building to enable the documents to be stored and cared for correctly. In 1918 the library was moved to Eastgate Street where it remains today to be used by researchers and family historians from all around the country.

The first William Salt Library, now Stafford Railway Building Society

[32] Further information about the life of William Salt is recorded in "William Salt and His Library" by Randle W. Knight.

Chapter 7
Harriet

When twins Thomas and Harriet Salt were born in May 1830, George IV was on the throne. Harriet would live to see Adolf Hitler as Führer of Germany. She died in December 1934, in Clevedon, on the Severn Estuary, 8 miles north east of Weston-super-Mare, where she had spent the last 57 years of her life. She never married.

Harriet appears on the 1841 and 1851 Census returns living with her father and younger sister, Sarah, at Weeping Cross. We are then unable to find any trace of her until she reappears on the 1881 Census, living in Clevedon.

On 22nd October, 1855 a young lady by the name of Harriet Salt, aged 25, arrived in New York from Liverpool on the ship, "Jeremiah Thompson". We have been unable to discover whether this is "our Harriet" or not. Did she travel round the world? Harriet arrived in Clevedon in 1877 and by 1881 she was living at "Firlands". This is where she remained for the rest of her life accompanied, for many of those years, by a German lady's maid, Francesco Sommer,

Firlands, Clevedon

Despite no longer living in Stafford, Harriet was a great benefactor to the Parish of Berkswich. Having been left £500 a year by her father, she was a wealthy woman who used some of her money to build an Infants' School in Walton.

The school was built next to the Vicarage in about 1870 to provide a basic education for children under the age of six or seven who were still too young to attend the Village School. Harriet's school existed until December 1891, when the government accepted responsibility for the education of all children. She maintained this school completely at her own expense for over twenty years. It had been run by just two mistresses; firstly Mrs Sarah Keeling, wife of the village postmaster, and then latterly by Mrs Hannah Pratt, a widow.

Every year Harriet would provide "Summer" and "Winter" Treats for the children who attended her school. At the end of the 1884 Summer Term the children, about 30 in total, were taken by Mrs Pratt to the home of Mrs Hand, which was situated opposite Weeping Cross House. They played in the large orchard, ran races, and enjoyed the swings that had been provided. Some older brothers and sisters joined the infants for tea and then, following a sing song, numerous presents provided by Harriet and Mrs Hand

Harriet Salt

were distributed to all the children. The "Treat" ended at 6 p.m. with three hearty cheers for Miss Salt and Mrs Hand.

The Winter Treat always took place as the children broke up for Christmas. After singing songs which they had learnt during the term, they were presented with a warm article of clothing. Prayers were said by the Vicar and then the children departed - each with a bun and an orange!

When the school closed, it was Harriet's wish that the building should be used as a Church Room, for Sunday School, mothers' meetings and educational classes. On New Year's Day 1892 the first "mothers meeting" was held in the school, but it appears that they were short of chairs! Twelve had been donated but there was a need for another dozen if mothers were not to sit on the floor!

The true extent of Harriet's generosity was not made clear until early in 1944. The Parish Magazine carried an obituary to Harry Tilstone written by Mrs Levett of

Milford Hall. Harry had worked at the Hall for many years, first as a carpenter and then a game keeper.

In 1871 eight year old Harry was a boarder with Mrs Sarah Keeling, at the Village Post Office and he is described as a scholar, presumably at Harriet's school or the Village School. Although the Census tells us that Harry was born in Staffordshire, the exact parish is recorded as "unknown". There were no other Tilstones in the Berkswich area at that time.

The Infants School, Walton, now a private house.

Harry must have shown considerable promise as a pupil. The obituary states that he was educated at the Woodard School at Denstone (now Denstone College) "by the wish of Miss Salt, sister of the late Sir Thomas Salt, as she was interested in the Tilstone family". Why she showed this interest we can't explain as there did not appear to be any other members of the Tilstone family working for the Salts or living in the area.

Although Harriet lived a long way from her twin brother and his family she kept in close contact with them. The boys attended Clifton College on the outskirts of Bristol, just twelve miles from their aunt's home, and often spent weekends and holidays with her.

Walter Petit Salt, her nephew, who was a Captain in the 2nd Lancashire Fusiliers, was killed in 1916. His name appears on the Clevedon Roll of Honour, his address is given as Firlands, Highfield Road, Clevedon.

Harriet was the oldest inhabitant of the town when she died in December 1934 at the age of 104. She was buried at All Saints, Clevedon.

Chapter 8
Social Life

Sarah Salt, Thomas' younger sister, had remained at Weeping Cross caring for her father and acting as mistress of the house. Following her father's death in March 1871, her brother Thomas and his family, moved from their home at Walton-on-the-Hill to Weeping Cross House. Sarah was now in a position to make a life for herself.

On the 27th September, 1873 she married the Reverend Percy Brent, son of Daniel Brent, Vicar of Grendon, Northants.

The bride was given away by her brother, and the Church at Walton was decorated with flowers to complement the pale lavender of the brides dress and the pink roses carried by the three bridesmaids.

Easton Maudit Church,

Although it was a Thursday, all the children from the village school congregated outside the church and as the happy couple left, they threw flowers in their path. Sarah would be missed in the Parish as she had been responsible for many acts of charity and kindness to her neighbours. The bride was forty, her husband twelve years her junior. At the time of the marriage, Percy was assistant curate to his father but in 1875 he was appointed Vicar in the nearby village of Easton Maudit.

Sarah and Percy had no children and after working for two years in Enfield, Middlesex, Percy returned north, as Vicar of Downton on Rock, Herefordshire. Their final move was to Westbury on Trim, Bristol.

It is clear that the Salt family were instigators of many local events held at

Rev. Percy Brent

Weeping Cross House, in the Village School or the Barley Mow. The social life of the area revolved around the landed gentry and the church.

Sarah Brent née Salt

On 19th April, 1882, Thomas and his family were present at the opening of the Sister Dora Convalescent Hospital on Cannock Chase. As Member of Parliament, it fell to Thomas to give an address thanking all those who had worked so hard to establish the hospital. The M.P. would also regularly present the prizes at the Village school with children gaining recognition for regular attendance and cleanliness!

Thomas presided at a meeting at the Barley Mow in July 1885 for the purpose of establishing a Benefit Club. Clubs such as these were set up to allow people to subscribe small amounts, on a weekly basis, into a scheme that would help them pay for medical care should they fall ill, be injured, or provide for their burial should they die! The meeting was not a success as the parishioners' especially the young men, were conspicuous by their absence. Thomas wondered if it had been worth his while making the journey from London to attend. At least he was able to give some publicity for his book published in 1868 called "How to Save Money and Keep it Safe, or Village Clubs and their Successors".

"The Soup Kitchen" at 2 Church Lane, Stafford, a charitable organisation, was started by Thomas and was mainly funded by contributions from him. The Soup Kitchen first appears in the Census returns in 1871. Times were hard and soup kitchens were being established all over the country to help provide some warm nourishment for the poor and long term unemployed. By 1901 the Soup Kitchen in Stafford remained in operation. However several teachers, presumably from the nearby St Mary's School, were lodging there[33]. In 1903 it became a boarding house for theatricals. Today it is the place to go for morning coffee or afternoon tea!

---

[33] 1901 Census

It was said that Sir Thomas would never let a wayfarer pass his door at Weeping Cross without them being assisted, if they wished, either with a soup ticket if they were travelling towards Stafford or with food if they were going towards Cannock or Lichfield.

Lady Salt and her helpers were also responsible for organising a local Blanket Club whereby people could subscribe a small amount each week. This money was used to purchase blankets which families were able to "borrow" when winter came. These had to be returned when the better weather arrived (washed!) and they would then be stored until the following winter. It is clear from entries in the Church Magazine that some families were reluctant to return their blankets when Spring arrived!

December 1885 saw a Concert in the Village School, organised by Mrs Salt and the Vicar's wife, Mrs Inge. The room was bursting at the seams and many people were unable to get inside to hear songs, stories, piano recitals and readings. Thomas and Helen had recruited the services of their future son-in-law, Joseph Lavies, to help with the entertainment. There was some criticism of the evening – too many "readings" and the event was too short! Another evening of entertainment was arranged for the end of February

The Soup Kitchen, Church Lane in 2009

with a promise that it would be an altogether comic affair. A profit of £3 16s 10d was donated to Walton Church.

Cricket was also a major event in the area with regular "Cricket Weeks" being held at Weeping Cross during August. Teams from Walton, Weeping Cross, Standon, Christ Church, Bednall and the Grammar School all competed. The Weeping Cross team was often "helped" to victory by university colleagues of the Salt boys, some of whom had played at County level and had certainly represented their university. Each day Mr & Mrs Salt provided tea for players and spectators. Lunch on Wednesday and supper on Thursday were the rewards for the players.

In 1889 Thomas was so busy as Member of Parliament and Chairman of Lloyds Bank that it was decided not to hold a formal cricket week. Instead it was agreed to organise a Ladies versus Gentlemen match! The gentlemen were permitted to use only their left hand, and were compelled to wear top hats at all times. If they lost the hat running after the ball, they had first to retrieve the hat before touching the ball. If they caught a lady whilst not wearing their headgear, it was "Not Out". Try running and catching a ball wearing a top hat! Despite all this, the gentlemen still managed to win! Mr and Mrs Salt dispensed their usual hospitality.[34] Mr Bernard Hand helped liven up the week by organising a picnic for everyone on Cannock Chase.

The two churches in the Parish were constantly in debt and Weeping Cross House was the site of many fund raising events. August 5th 1896 saw a "Sale of Work" in the house while, outside, games such as "Chalking the Pig's Eye" kept the visitors amused. The real attraction however was a "Bicycle Gymkhana" believed to be the first such event in the area. No doubt the Twigg children who lived just across the Cannock Road from Weeping Cross House took part!

The Twigg Children

The drawing room of Weeping Cross House was often the meeting point for those doing good works in the parish and further afield. In 1898 Sir Thomas and Lady Salt hosted a gathering to raise funds for the Missions to Seamen. The Rev. S.M. Young, Chaplain to the Port of Manchester, gave a talk about the work being done on a new steamer around the Bristol Channel, South Wales and the South West of England. The steamer had a room fitted out like a chapel and they were therefore able to hold services for officers and men on board as they were often far too busy to go to church once their ships had docked. After the talk tea was served in the billiard room and £10 4s 8d was collected for the cause.

---

[34] Berkswich Parish Magazine 1889

Another meeting at Weeping Cross House was held in January 1903 at which the ladies discussed the advisability of employing a Nurse for the Parish. With Lady Salt in the Chair, it was agreed that the opinion of the parishioners should be sought. If sufficient people were interested, a nurse would be recruited. The nurse would attend maternity cases, but no infectious cases, because of a risk of passing disease on to other patients. A scale of subscriptions was drawn up as follows:-

Class	Subscription	Fees	
Cottagers	1/- per year	2/-	For Nurse per week
Artisan	2/- per year	3/-	Ditto
Farmers	2/6 per year	3/6	Ditto
Gentry	10/- per year	10/-	Ditto

There was a further scale of charges for those who did not subscribe, and one for occasional visits for dressing wounds etc. It was agreed to hold another meeting on 15th February, and all parishioners were asked to inform Mrs Levett at Milford Hall if they were willing to subscribe. In due course a Parish Nurse, Mrs Smith, was appointed.

Summer afternoons would often find the Salt family and their friends out for a picnic, on the canal, in their steam boat, the "Dolly Varden". As Thomas disliked being held up at locks, he would often offer a shilling to those in front of him so that he could jump the queue and continue his "cruise". The locals soon got wise to this and, if it looked like the sort of afternoon that the Salts would be out for a sail, they would assemble in their boats by the locks awaiting the arrival of the "Dolly Varden" and the opportunity to earn a shilling. Of course, if the Salt family embarked at Radford Bank there was no guarantee as to which direction they would travel in!

The "Dolly Varden" was eventually given by the Salt family to the North Staffordshire Railway Company as a Canal Inspection Launch. It was in time destroyed by the Railway! Thomas was appointed Deputy Chairman of the North Staffordshire Railway in 1875 - a post he held for three years before resigning. It is believed that there was a clash of personalities between Thomas and the then Chairman, Minton Campbell! Campbell resigned in August 1883 because of his failing health and Thomas was appointed Chairman in his place. This was a post he would hold until his death.

In 1898 Thomas resigned as Chairman of Lloyds bank, although he remained a director. During his time as Chairman the bank had flourished with its assets growing from 11 million to 40 million pounds in twelve years. The following year, 1899, Thomas was elected as one of the first Aldermen of Staffordshire County Council. He was also a Trustee and Honorary Treasurer of Staffordshire General Infirmary.

In 1894 the family decided to enlarge Weeping Cross House by adding an extension to both ends of the building. "Le Petit Salon" was built at right angles to the entrance hall specifically to hold the paintings of the Rev. John Louis Petit, uncle of Thomas. Almost 300 pictures, mainly studies in browns and greys, covered every inch of the walls, whilst a soft light coming from the fanlight in the roof showed the paintings to their best advantage.

At the opposite end of the house, the extension would create a work room, and a store room with two bedrooms above. This extension was destroyed by fire in 1926.[35]

Sir Thomas Salt in "Le Petit Salon" surrounded by the paintings of Rev J.L. Petit.

---

[35] See Chapter on Baswich House School

The Plans and the finished building at the east end of the main house

Chapter 9
Celebrations and Sadness

The children of Thomas and Helen were destined to make good marriages.

Laura was the first daughter to walk down the aisle, and she married Ernest Pollock, who would eventually become Master of the Rolls, one of the country's senior judges. The service took place on Easter Tuesday, 12th April 1887 at St Saviour's Church, St George's Square, London and was conducted by the Rector of Chislehurst, Rev, F.H. Murray, Rev. W. Haig-Brown, Headmaster of Charterhouse School, where the groom was a student, and Rev. F.G. Inge, Vicar of Berkswich.

Berkswich Parish Magazine records that Miss Salt would be greatly missed from Sunday school as she kept the largest class in splendid order! It was also stated that the groom devoted some of his spare time to the "Charterhouse Mission" in Tabard Street, London.

The Mission was set up, funded, and in some cases staffed, by old boys of Charterhouse School. It was established as part of a movement where relatively privileged members of society moved into poor areas of the country and worked to alleviate poverty.

To ensure funds were available for new projects the Old Carthusians Society would put on balls, concerts and dramas. Those lucky enough to attend were encouraged to dig deep into their pockets.

The Dining Room, Judges Lodgings, Stafford

Laura and Ernest met for the first time on 28th January, 1884 as a result of a fire in the Judges' Lodgings in the centre of Stafford. The Assizes were taking place in the Shire Hall with Mr Baron Huddleston and Mr Justice Manisty holding court. Ernest was Marshal to Mr Justice Manisty. At just gone noon the alarm was raised, when Mr Hard, the chef de cuisine attached to the Judges retinue, noticed smoke coming from the eaves of the building. He had been busy preparing for that evenings dinner, at which the Judges and their families were scheduled to entertain the members of the Bar in their Lodgings.

The flames were rapidly gaining hold in the roof timbers. The Deputy Chief Constable inspected the second floor rooms while the flames raged above him. He immediately ordered the servants to remove all the furniture so that there was nothing to burn within the rooms, while others, including the Judges' Marshals carried buckets of water up two flights of stairs, in an attempt to douse the fire. Although the Volunteer Fire Brigade arrived promptly, there was some delay as the men wanted some assurance that they would be paid! The water had to be pumped from the River Sow some 500 yards away with a hose that was old and split in several places. As the fire gained hold there was a real fear that it

Ernest Pollock

would spread into the adjoining Shire Hall, so telegrams were sent to Ingestre and Wolverhampton asking for assistance. Lord Shrewsbury drove his steam fire engine from Ingestre and after a journey taking an hour and a half the brigade arrived from Wolverhampton. Fortunately, by the time both parties arrived the fire was under control. This did not prevent the Chief Constable of Wolverhampton sending a bill for his Fire Brigade's expenses to Stafford! The fire had demolished the greater part of the roof of the east wing and three bedrooms were open to the sky. There was also considerable damage to the second floor.

Thomas Salt, on hearing of the devastation, immediately offered accommodation to the Judges and their Marshals at his home at Weeping Cross. It was on this occasion that Laura was to meet her future husband. Her brother, Herbert, was eventually to marry the grand-daughter of Mr Justice Manisty.

The Judge's Lodgings were covered with a tarpaulin on the evening of 28th January but the following day, which was a Sunday, workmen moved in to remove the debris and make good the damage. By Monday evening the Judges were able to return to their lodgings!

The report of the fire in the Stafford Chronicle, 2nd February, 1884, concludes with the words "The town of Stafford will never be secure against devastating conflagrations and possible loss of life without a steam fire engine and a well arranged system of hydrants". If only the powers that be had taken note of this comment perhaps the dreadful fire in 1887 that destroyed an Elizabethan timbered house in Gaolgate Street, would not have happened.

The Judge's Lodgings built 1802

Mary Louisa was the next to marry in January 1889 at the age of twenty-one. Her husband was Joseph H. Lavies, the son of J.S. Lavies, a distinguished London doctor. Dr Lavies had been ill for some time and died shortly before the wedding but it was his wish that the ceremony should go ahead as planned. The Staffordshire Advertiser records that the groom's father had been a member of the choir of Westminster Abbey on the occasion of Queen Victoria's Coronation!

The marriage service took place at the old Parish Church, Chislehurst, the church where the bride's parents had been married twenty seven years earlier and it was conducted by the same minister, the Rev. F.H. Murray, assisted by the brother of the groom, Rev. B. Lavies.

Although the celebrations were overshadowed by the recent death of Dr. Lavies it was a happy occasion. Many relations travelled from Victoria station to Bickley, the nearest station to Chislehurst, in a special saloon carriage. The church still had the Christmas decorations in place and, to complement them, the two bridesmaids carried bouquets of Christmas roses, myrtle and holly berries. After the service the wedding party was entertained to afternoon tea at the Rectory. At 4.30 the bride and groom left to catch the train to Folkestone where they were to spend a short honeymoon at the Pavilion Hotel. The remainder of the wedding party returned to London where the younger members of the family visited the Adelphi Theatre to watch a performance of "The Silver Falls", a melodrama. A telegram arrived at the theatre to inform the family that Mr & Mrs Lavies had arrived safely in Folkestone!

This was the happy start to a marriage, which would be short, and end in the early death of both parties.

Over nine years later on 30th September, 1896, it was the turn of Helen Salt to marry Mr J. Cecil McFerran. Helen had been born at Walton and this may have been the reason for her wedding taking place in the village church. This episode is recorded in the Church Magazine. "It is the event which has been looked forward to for some time past and many had been the hopes expressed that it might be a fine day. The greater part of the day before, which had been spent by many willing friends in decorating the church and village, had been dull. Wednesday morning dawned with a thick fog, which gradually turned to brilliant sunshine as the day wore on. For the bride and groom, and a few near relations and friends, the day began with a celebration of Holy Communion at 8 o'clock in the morning. A few minutes before two, by the Walton Church clock, the bride accompanied by her father entered the church. After the service about 160 guests were hospitably entertained at Weeping Cross by Mr & Mrs Salt. There were several arches between Walton and Weeping Cross, all bearing marks of the affection shown to Mr and Mrs Salt and their daughter by the entire parish. The bride and groom left for Church Stretton shortly after 4.00 p.m."

Less than a year later yet another Salt wedding was to take place, this time in London, but before then there were other celebrations in the family. Her Majesty, Queen Victoria made Thomas Salt a baronet in her birthday honours list on 3rd June 1899.

Shire Hall, Stafford

This announcement caused great excitement in the town and within days a group of local worthies held a meeting in the Swan Hotel to make arrangements for a celebration. The Victorians did not hang about when organising such an event.

On 20th June, less than three weeks from the date of the original announcement of his baronetcy, the Shire Hall was filled with friends and supporters of Sir Thomas. Representatives from all the organisations with which he was connected were present.

The tables were decorated with flowers and plants, the gift of the Chairman of the County Council, the Earl of Harrowby who could not be present, as he was recuperating at a health resort! Sir Thomas served on the County Council as an

Alderman and was a close friend of the Earl. Flags and bunting along with the Union flag and the Stars and Stripes decorated the room.

The food, a splendid spread, was prepared by the staff of the Vine Hotel who dashed backwards and forwards between the Shire Hall and the Public House carrying plates of food and wine. The landlord, Mr T. Bennett made sure that everything went according to plan.

The evening, fully reported in the Staffordshire Advertiser, was an evening of speeches in honour and praise of the town's former M.P. The ladies were not invited!

The "Advertiser" however, commented on the fact that, although many speeches were made, no mention was given to the work Sir Thomas had done to bring his uncle's collection of books and documents to the town to form the William Salt Library. The article goes on to say " It may not perhaps be known to every reader of the Staffordshire Advertiser that the William Salt Library was established for the purpose of preserving whatever documentary material should prove worthy of preservation towards a complete and, as far as possible, satisfactory history of the county of Stafford, including records of its manorial properties and their descent from age to age, memorials of its worthy and distinguished families, its political, religious, and social life, the architecture of its churches, abbeys, castles and other edifices, its natural productions, manufacturers, local customs, folk-lore, and whatever else may be of interest to any and every section of the population, for surely everyone must be interested in some branch or other of this comprehensive scheme. It remains to say that owing to various causes the slender endowment of the William Salt Library is in great need of being strengthened. The books are becoming worn and broken, new bindings are necessary for some of its valuable printed and manuscript volumes, while new books are often desirable; cases, too, are needed for the ancient deeds, and a suitable cabinet for seals and similar valuables. In short, the burden of this invaluable institution should no longer be permitted to rest on the shoulders of a few generous and philanthropic individuals, but should be taken up by the county at large, so that it may fulfil to the utmost the purpose for which, by the liberality of the Salt family, it was originally founded."

George Edmund Stevenson Salt

A month later, on 25th July the Salts' second son was to marry at Christ Church, Lancaster Gate, London. Miss Ethel Manisty, youngest daughter of Mr Henry

Manisty, of 52 Lancaster Gate, was married to Mr Herbert Salt, son of Sir Thomas Salt, Bart. of Weeping Cross, Stafford.

The wedding ring was specially made from gold dug up by the bridegroom on his Californian property. Herbert had originally set sail for Dakota in April 1893 with the intention of becoming a rancher but finally settled in California, becoming a fruit farmer.

Although there was a host of handsome wedding presents, including some costly articles of plate and jewellery from relations and friends in Staffordshire and London, there was also an unusual number of cheques given, owing to the difficulty of taking presents in kind to California.

Things did not turn out as the couple intended. Their life in California was difficult and eventually after a disastrous harvest and the failure of the orange crop they returned to England, living at Weeping Cross while they saved money to buy furniture! Some time later Herbert inherited "Henlade" a property near Taunton and as a result he changed his name by deed poll to Anderdon, his mother's maiden name.

A new century always seems like a new beginning but the first two years of the twentieth century brought great sadness to the family. 1900 started badly with the death of the Salt's son-in-law, Joseph Lavies, on 23rd February after a short and very severe attack of pneumonia. Although Joseph died at his home in London his body was brought back to Stafford to be buried in Baswich Church. Only six weeks later the Salts were to lose a son.

George Edmund Stevenson Salt was the third son of Sir Thomas and Lady Salt, born in February 1873. At 21 he was a Second Lieutenant and then in March 1898 he was promoted to Lieutenant in the Royal Welsh Fusiliers. Within six months the Boer War had broken out and he had to go and fight.

G.E.S. Salt's Grave in South Africa

Salt's battalion set off for South Africa on the troopship "Oriental" on 22nd October 1899, arriving at the Cape on 13th November. They were sent on to Durban, and along with the 2nd Royal Fusiliers, 2nd Royal Scots Fusiliers, and 2nd Royal Irish Fusiliers, formed the 6th Brigade under Major General Barton. The Battalion arrived on 18th November 1899 at Mooi River, resting until 26th November. They then marched to Estcourt, a distance of 23 miles, taking 7 hours to cover the distance.

George wrote home regularly and after his death the family published his letters in a small book.[36] On 14th March, 1900 he wrote, "I feel much fitter after the change I have had and am ready to pursue the wily Boer again. They are holding positions in the Biggersberg Mountains, and I expect we shall move against them before long. My pony is well, but this is a very bad time of year for them, and they are terribly lazy."

Just five days later he wrote again, "Since last writing to you I have received three parcels, one containing shirts and socks for the men, and the others raisins, nibs, suit of pyjamas, and all kinds of little things – all very useful. I have now such a supply of things that I cannot carry any more and have had to give a great many clothes away: and, as everybody else is in much the same state, do not send me any more parcels just yet.

Royal Welch Fusiliers. G.E.S. Salt is believed to be 3rd from right seated.

I am in hospital with an attack of fever. On Friday I felt good for little and worse on Saturday, so in the evening I saw our doctor who sent me to bed. I got up and stood in the doorway of my tent, but immediately collapsed backwards on to my bed. My temperature was still high so I was despatched to the Field Hospital about 8 miles away."

George's last letter home is dated 21st March. This is followed by a letter from a fellow officer informing his parents that George is suffering from enteric fever. Yet another letter from this same officer reads, "Long before you get this letter you will have heard of the sad death of your son. When I wrote last week he seemed to be doing so well, and only to have a mild attack, but that evening we were told he was much worse. He became delirious and never really regained consciousness. From time to time he seemed to be a little better, and all hoped that, with his excellent

---

[36] WSL Letters and Diary of Lt. G.E.S. Salt

constitution, he would pull through. Last night, however, he quite suddenly became very much worse, and Major Daly came over about 8 'clock to say that he was afraid there was no hope. Kington, Hurt and I went over to the hospital to find out if we could do anything. We stayed for some time, and would have liked to stay until the end, but the doctors did not wish us to do this, as there were four other cases in the same ward, one of which was very serious. The clergyman held a very short service and then we came away.

Early this morning we went over, hoping against hope, to inquire, and found that he had passed away peacefully and quietly in his sleep at twenty minutes to four this morning. The funeral is to take place this afternoon. He will lie in a corner of the little cemetery, about half a mile from camp. We are going to put a wooden cross for the present, and a low rail round the grave. There is a stone wall running round the ground, so there will be no danger of it being disturbed. It is so sad that he never heard that General Buller had mentioned him in despatches."

January 1901 saw the death of Queen Victoria and the country was plunged into a period of mourning with all adults wearing black and even iron railings getting a fresh coat of black paint. However, the new King, Edward VII, in his wisdom declared that mourning for his mother should only last three months, but the year continued to bring more heartache to the Salt family.

Following the death of her husband, Mary Lavies had not been well and so she came home to Stafford to spend time with her parents prior to undergoing surgery. She was resident at Weeping Cross House on the night of 31st March when the 1901 Census was taken. Shortly after this she returned to London with her nurse and underwent an operation from which she appeared to be recovering well. Three weeks after her operation she had a relapse and died on 21st May at the age of 33. Her body was returned to Stafford and she was buried with her husband in Baswich churchyard. Suffering from an attack of bronchitis, Sir Thomas was unable to attend his daughter's funeral.

On 19th June 1901, less than a month after his sister's funeral, Mr Reginald John Salt of Thermalito California, fourth son, of Sir Thomas Salt of Weeping Cross, Stafford was married to

Mary Lavies née Salt

55

Miss Maud Fanny Wigram, youngest daughter of Mr Robert Wigram of Longcroft, Banstead, Surrey.

Reginald, like his brother Herbert, also returned to England from California and eventually became the Manager of Lloyds Bank in Leamington Spa!

Sir Thomas's daughters were now all married and settled down but he would not live to see his eldest son and heir walk down the aisle with his bride.

Chapter 10
Changes

1904 Sir Thomas had been suffering from a bad attack of flu but, with the better weather, he appeared to be making good progress. Attended by Dr Reid the local doctor, no one was unduly worried by his illness. He had been out in a Bath chair viewing his estate on Tuesday, but by Wednesday evening he had taken a turn for the worse. He gradually faded away and eventually died at twenty past ten on Friday morning the 8th April, just one month before his 74th birthday.

The news of his death quickly spread. Flags were flown at half-mast throughout Stafford, and a muffled peal was rung on the bells of St Mary's church.

The funeral was fixed for two o'clock on Tuesday the 12th and it was the family's wish that it should be a quiet, simple affair, with only family flowers. Sir Thomas had been held in high esteem by many of the poor and needy whom he had helped over the years. Women, grateful for his help in the past, walked from Stafford carrying their babies in their arms and by two o'clock the church was full, with many people standing outside awaiting the funeral party and anxious to pay their final respects.

With the exception of Lady Salt and her daughters, all the mourners, including the estate workers and household servants, walked from Weeping Cross along Baswich Lane to the Church where the family had been regular worshippers. The coffin, covered by a purple pall on which was a simple cross of flowers from the family, was received into church by the Vicar, the Rev F.G. Inge, the Curate, the Rev J.L. Cappell, and the Rev. Edward Salt, cousin of Sir Thomas. The service was plain, short, and without music. His body was interred at the side of his daughter Mary's grave and close to the cross in memory of his son George who is buried in South Africa.

Baswich Lane as it looked in 1904

Lady Salt at Weeping Cross

Major Thomas Anderdon Salt of the 11th Hussars was now the second Baronet of Standon and Weeping Cross and he, of course, inherited the family home. Thomas was due to be married within the year, and the now Dowager Lady Salt decided that she must make her home elsewhere to allow the newly weds to move into Weeping Cross House. Should she move to her home in London, or look for something more local and close to her many friends?

Before long Lady Salt had made a decision about her future. She would buy the house in Walton on the Hill that had been her home when she was first married and where at least two of her children had been born. Soon after her marriage to Thomas in 1860, they had leased the house from the Earl of Lichfield. On 20th March 1871 they agreed a further 21 year lease with the Earl, but, unfortunately, the following day Thomas's father died. A sub lease was, therefore, entered into between Thomas Benson Elley, a shoe manufacturer, and Thomas Salt. The Elley family were to remain at Walton on the Hill for several years. [37]

Lady Salt's House at Walton on the Hill

---

[37] WSL D1716/13/23 & D1716/13/14

In January 1905 Lady Salt bought the estate at Walton, which included No 1 The Village and Congreve House along with several acres of land, from the Earl of Lichfield. This was to remain her home until 1920 when she moved to Chelsea.

The marriage of Sir Thomas and Miss Nora Wiggin, youngest daughter of Mr H.A. Wiggin of Walton Hall Eccleshall, took place at Chebsey Church on Tuesday, 17th January 1905. Due to the family still being in mourning[38], only a few close relatives were present at the church, although there were many local residents waiting outside the building for a glimpse of the bride. The whole countryside was covered in snow but the sun shone brightly as the couple emerged from church, and the bells rang out across the surrounding fields. Nora was attended by four bridesmaids dressed in white silk with skirts trimmed with a deep band of plain blue velvet, and with sashes to match. After a reception at Walton Hall, which was attended by a great number of friends, the couple left for London at 4 o'clock, before travelling on to Corsica for the start of their honeymoon.

Nora Wiggin, dressed not for her wedding, but to be presented at Court

Nora was soon pregnant. Her husband was somewhat dismayed that they had to return to England earlier than he had intended, as Nora could no longer cope with the travelling.

Once back in England it became clear that Sir Thomas Anderdon Salt was not quite as fond of the family house, built by his grandfather, as his parents had been. He wanted something larger and grander. He was competing with their great friends the Fitzherberts of Swynnerton Hall! By January 1906 Weeping Cross House had been put on the market. A letter from the Estate Manager at Standon, Mr W. Sillito, dated 15th January to estate agents, Nock & Joseland of 48 Queen Street, Wolverhampton stated "I now send you printed particulars of Weeping Cross House Estate. The price required for the same by Sir Thomas A. Salt, Bart. is £7,500 net. In offering the property to your clients please add in to that sum such commission as you require for effecting the sale."[39]

These sale particulars describe the property in great detail. One thing that was obviously very important to the landed gentry at the time was the fact that the house was within easy reach by road or rail of the meetings of three Packs of Hounds, viz:- The North Staffordshire, The South Staffordshire and The Albrighton.

---

[38] Widows were expected to wear full mourning for two years. Everyone else presumably suffered less – for children mourning parents or vice versa the period of time was one year.
[39] WA   D-NAJ/C/1/SA1

The sale details provide what would appear to be the first descriptive account of the house, as it had never before been put on the open market. It is worth reproducing this document as it enables us to look back at an age before the First World War when life was somewhat different from today.

The House is described as "a First-class Moderate-sized Country Residence standing in a high and healthy situation, and surrounded by well-stocked gardens, thickly shrubbed grounds and park-like land.

The Drive and Entrance Lodge

The Residence is approached from the Entrance Lodge by a short winding carriage drive, bordered with shrubs and trees. It is a three-storeyed red-brick Mansion of a pleasing style, with high pitched roof and numerous gables. It was erected and fitted in a substantial manner, regardless of cost, and is in first-class order and repair.

It contains a square Entrance Hall partly panelled in old oak; handsome Dining-room with polished-oak floor and panelled walls and ceiling, communicating with a Serving Lobby and also with a Conservatory; Drawing-room with polished-oak floor, panelled wall, and massive oak mantel-piece handsomely carved; Library with fitted solid oak book-cases, and contains two fire-places and five windows; Billiard Room and there is also a Gunroom, an Office-room, and a burglar-proof Strongroom.

There are seven principal bedrooms and a dozen smaller Bedrooms and Dressing-rooms; also a Linen-room, Housemaids' Closet, Housemaids' Sinks, Boxroom etc. The domestic offices comprise a Housekeeper's Room, Store-room, good Kitchen, Serving Lobby, Butler's Pantry, Larder, Servants' Hall, Scullery, etc. The Cellars are dry, spacious and airy.

There are three Bathrooms (two of which contain Water-closets); also five separate Water-closets. Electric Light, Electric Bells and Hot-water Heating

Apparatus are fitted throughout the house. Gas and high-pressure Water Supply are taken from the Stafford Town mains, which adjoin the property. There is a good modern drainage system, an Electric-light house, with powerful Gas Engine and a separate Accumulator House, Carpenter's Shop, Paint Shop, Boiler-house, Slaughter-house, Potato-house, Fruit-house, Granary, Barn, Stick-shed, Lofts etc.

There are well-built Stables and Loose-boxes for ten horses; good coach-house, and Living-rooms for coachman over the stable; harness-room, with Bedroom for groom, and separate Bedroom for two men servants over the loose-boxes

There are ample Flower Gardens and Pleasure Grounds; three walled-in Kitchen Gardens, an Orchard, two Greenhouses, Vinery, Peach-house etc; large Shrubberies, with small woods and plantations and numerous walks therein.

There is also a good Laundry, with Living Cottage thereto; a separate Garden Cottage, a Farm Bailiff's Cottage, a range of wooden Farm Buildings and Piggeries, Detached Dairy, Dutch Hay-barns, Manure-shed, Cattle-sheds, Poultry-houses and Dog Kennels.

Looking towards Weeping Cross House from the Estate

Lying within the grounds of the Mansion (but quite walled off there-from and having a separate entrance from the public Main Road,) is a Detached Smaller Residence, containing two Reception-rooms, seven Bed and Dressing Rooms, Bathroom, two Water-closets, ample domestic offices, Stabling for three horses, Loose-box, Coach-house, and good sized Garden and Grounds.

Immediate possession can be had of the Mansion and of the smaller Detached Residence, with all stabling thereto, and of the gardens, glass-houses, orchard, shrubberies, woods and plantations; also of the Entrance Lodge, Gardener's

Cottage, Laundry Cottage and Workshops. Possession of the 27 acres of Farm Land, Bailiff's Cottage and all Farm buildings can be had on September 29th 1906".[40]

Mr Percy Smith who was born at Radford Bank recalls the estate in his memoirs. "The farm was self-contained with buildings for cows, horses, and pigs and a barn. It has a dairy, run most efficiently by Mrs Dix, which was smartly tiled in white and had a settle - a long, wide shelf on which large pans of milk were put to rest so that the cream could be skimmed off. Mrs Dix, the wife of the farm manager, Mr Hamlet Dix, made butter and cream cheese if there was a surplus of milk, particularly in early summer when the grass was lush. Milk was delivered to households along Weeping Cross by a man called, if I remember correctly, Will Edwards. He carried a yoke across his shoulders with a bucket on each end, and a measure to ladle out the milk into the customers' jugs. Sometimes there were surplus vegetables from the large walled garden, and these would be for sale at the dairy.

The land was interspersed with specially planted spinneys and all about were individual trees - sycamore, oak, ash, lime, willow, red and white chestnut, poplar, elm, hawthorn, Scots pine and a row of rare Deodar Fir trees along the eastern boundary. Under these trees the gamekeeper bred pheasants and partridges in runs. There was a sturdy board fence on the western boundary (near what is Bridle Road today) to deter poachers. The fields were mainly bounded by wrought-iron palings. A small, puddled pond, which filled from land drains, was partially bordered by rhododendrons. This pond had a little island in the middle and there was a wooden boathouse with a corrugated iron roof, where a small boat was kept. There were gravel drives around the estate where the family could walk or ride in a pony cart."

No doubt the Estate Agent, Nock & Joseland, entrusted with the job of selling the estate would have been looking forward to a lucrative payout once the property was sold. However, it was not to be. On 7th February, 1906 they received a further letter from William Sillito, Estate Manager, stating "We have just received an offer for this property (from a gentleman in North Staffordshire who approached us last July) which we shall probably accept so please do not negotiate with anyone at the moment." [41]

Sir Thomas Anderdon Salt and his bride were to build a new house at Standon. It was not until July 1911 that the house was ready for them to move into. Set in 24 acres of land and designed by Liverpool architect J,F. Doyles it had oak panelling in many of the rooms together with beautiful carved fireplaces and cost a staggering £60,000, a tremendous amount for that time. Eventually it became clear that this house was too large and too expensive to run. In 1920 the family left Staffordshire and moved to Dorset.

---

[40] WA D-NAJ/C/1/SA1
[41] WA D-NAJ/C/1/SA1

Chapter 11
The New Family at Weeping Cross

The gentleman from North Staffordshire who eventually bought Weeping Cross House was William Morton Philips, Chairman of J and N Philips and Co Ltd of Manchester and Tean, Staffordshire. The company was established by John (1724-1803) and Nathaniel (1726-1808), second and third sons of John Philips of Tean and Checkley, Staffordshire, as "smallware" manufacturers and tape weavers in Tean in 1747. The business flourished and, where once weavers worked at home in their small cottages, the brothers brought all their workers into the new modern mill at Tean where they were able to work more efficiently.

This, of course, caused problems for the working mothers as they now required someone to care for their children whilst they were at work. The brothers decided to create what may well have been the first crèche in the country, employing nurses to look after the young children and babies within the mill itself. They also built a school for the older children. Many of the cottages in the village were built and owned by the company. The workers were well treated and therefore loyal to the company and the family.

The company continued to thrive and expand, buying up other companies within North Staffordshire and Greater Manchester, until the firm of J. and N. Philips became the headquarters of a nationwide merchanting and manufacturing enterprise. Mr Morton Philips, the fifth generation of the Philips family to run the company, became a very wealthy man.[42]

Upper Tean Mills

Morton's first visit to Weeping Cross was on 11th March 1905. Lady Salt took him over a good deal of the house and, after tea, he was shown around the outbuildings and the estate.

By 10th June 1905, Lady Salt had moved into her new home at Walton on the Hill. Morton and his wife Kate were invited to lunch, after which they drove over to Weeping Cross in the "Victoria", as Kate was rather delicate, and riding in the carriage was less fatiguing than walking. That night Morton wrote in his diary "There

---

[42] J. and N. Philips and Co. Ltd. closed in 1970.

are many drawbacks, but the accommodation would do for us, just. The situation is bad and there is no shooting. On the other hand the neighbourhood is good."

Time passed, and the Morton Philips family were still unsure about purchasing the house. There was some bother about "sanitary matters" that would cost about £350 to correct!

Eventually a conclusion was arrived at; they would move to Weeping Cross, but rent the house rather than buy it. The planned move helped Morton make a brave decision. On 16th May 1906 he wrote "I have taken the plunge and ordered the motor car. I look upon it as a necessity at Weeping Cross. I only hope that we shall get a satisfactory Chauffeur."

William Morton Philips

Just before Christmas 1906, the family eventually moved into their new home which, by now, was described as warm and comfortable. They soon settled in, and by August 1907 Morton decided he would like to buy the house after all.

It was not until 7th January 1908 that the property was eventually sold. It would appear that Sir T.A. Salt requested that, should the property come on to the market again, he would have a period of three months to decide whether or not he wished to buy it back.[43]

Percy Smith tells us that Mr Philips was the first person at Weeping Cross to own a motor-car. A Daimler Limousine had replaced the brougham, although the brougham still came out on lovely summer days. The acquisition of an automobile meant employing a chauffeur (in those days all car owners had to have one to deal with the snorting monsters.) When children from Weeping Cross were walking to school in Stafford they would see Mr Sawyer, the chauffeur, taking his master to catch the Manchester train.

They all knew Mr Sawyer, as he had a fine baritone voice and sang every Sunday in Baswich Church choir. As he passed them, he would give a cheery wave, and, if he was in the car rather than the brougham, he would sound the klaxon as a friendly greeting! The children would see him again as they walked home at teatime. He was now returning to Stafford station to meet his master off the early evening train. In those far off days, school lunch times were of 2 hours duration so that children finally went home some time between 4 & 5 o'clock.

The brougham and the Daimler were kept in the coach house at Weeping Cross and it was fascinating for the children to sneak in and watch Mr Sawyer

---

[43] WA D-NAJ/C/1/SA1

washing the vehicles and polishing the brass work. The carriage lamps had thick candles in them, which would often blow out in the wind; the horses then had to be brought to a halt so that the candles could be re-lit. The motorcar had paraffin lamps, with wide wicks, which had to be trimmed after use to minimise the smoke as it was necessary to keep the glass sparkling and clean.

Morton and his wife Kate, née Stopford, (reputed by the family to be a terrible snob) had six children. By the time they moved into Weeping Cross House, Mary, the eldest daughter was already married and Mark was making his own way in the world. Two girls, Christobel, and Rosamond were at home while Humphrey was away much of the time at Eton College. The youngest daughter Joan Letitia had died from scarlet fever in 1900 at the age of 8.

**From L to R Christobel, Morton, Mary, Humphrey, Kate, Mark
Seated Joan and Rosamund**

The Morton Philips family soon became part of the community, regularly attending church and supporting local events, both financially and with their presence. Mrs Morton Philips became the President of the Berkswich and Tixall Nursing Association, started by Lady Salt in 1903, and meetings of the committee were regularly held at Weeping Cross.

They continued many of the traditions that had been introduced by Sir Thomas and Lady Salt, with the exception of the regular cricket weeks. It would appear that the Morton Philips family were not keen to have their lawns destroyed by amateur sportsmen!

Gladys Pierce, however, wrote in 1913 of the annual school treat: "On Tuesday, June 10th, Mr and Mrs Morton Philips again very kindly gave us a School Treat.

We assembled with our teachers at Weeping Cross at 4 p.m. and marched to the large open motor shed, where tea was laid for us. We did ample justice to the good things provided. When tea was over we moved to the large field in the grounds; the boys to cricket, and we girls to the swings, where we enjoyed ourselves until the ladies and gentlemen came to us. We then went on the lawns and had games with Aunt Sally, races - flat, three-legged, and sack, - and Tugs-of-War. The winners were rewarded each with a bag of sweets and the losers watched us eat them. At the close we all scrambled for sweets, so that every child had the opportunity of having some. We then drew up in lines and gave hearty cheers to Mr and Mrs Morton Philips and family for their kindness; also for those who had cut up for us and waited upon us. As we marched off home we each had a cup of lemonade and a bun, and thus a most enjoyable afternoon and evening - which we shall never forget - came to a close."[44]

Mark Hibbert Philips

On 28th May 1914, the family were in London for a family wedding. Their daughter, Rosamond, was to marry Mr Jasper More, son of the late Robert Jasper More, a former Shropshire M.P., at St Peter's Church, Pimlico. It was a very grand affair, attended by the great and the good, including several Stafford people, the Dowager Lady Salt, with her daughter and son-in-law, Mr & Mrs McFerran, and the Levett family from Milford Hall. The teachers and pupils of Berkswich School sent the happy couple a silver vase.

Within three months, all their lives would be changed. Most of the young men who attended the wedding would be fighting in France and many would not return. Dowager Lady Salt would lose a son and two grandsons.[45]

Just two weeks after Rosamond's wedding, Mark the eldest son, dealt his father a heavy blow. On 11th June 1914 Morton wrote: "It was after 5 when Mark came to me and said I was to prepare for a shock, and then told me that he had married on the 7th March a girl of 21. A Roman

---

[44] Berkswich Parish Magazine 1913
[45] Walter Petit Salt D. 24/10/1916, Maurice A. McFerran D 21/3/1918.
Charles Thomas Anderdon Pollock D. 31/3/1918.

Catholic, without a penny and that a baby was expected in December. I hope and believe that is the worst though I know from sad experience that he would tell me any lie. I cannot trust myself to write about it. He has incurred a big debt which really tries me just now, but that is the least of the horrors. It was bad enough before, but this blackens my outlook on life. I hardly feel I can bear it." It was not until the following day that Morton found the strength to break the news to his wife and the rest of the family.

Mark had chosen to marry Eileen O'Sullivan-Beare, an Irish girl and their baby, a girl, was born in Ireland. For a while Mark and family were estranged from his parents. Eventually, as his father came to terms with the marriage, the rift was partially healed and the young family were sent to Australia where Mark was to work on behalf of the family business. A second daughter, Maureen, was born in Australia and at the time of writing, she is still alive, living in a nunnery in the south of England. She has been a nun since the age of 20.

After a year the family returned to England and along with many other young men Mark joined the forces.

Soon the Philips family's time at Weeping Cross was to come to an end. John W. Philips, father of Morton, who was born in 1827, died leaving the family house, "Heybridge" at Tean to his son. It was time to move on but, before Weeping Cross House could go on the open market a letter was sent to Sir Thomas Anderdon Salt, who was stationed in Rouen, giving him the opportunity to re-purchase his family home. A reply soon came back giving permission for the house to be sold.

Plan to accompany 1915 Sale Documents

The sale of the house was handled by Evans & Evans of Stafford, and an auction was scheduled for 4 p.m. on Saturday, 15th May, 1915 at their premises in Stafford. The estate now comprised over 41 acres, four cottages, two of which were newly built, a further detached house with garden, and capital stabling and farm buildings. The brochure states that "Shooting and Fishing can be found in the neighbourhood and the social amenities of the district are in every way desirable. Telegrams are delivered from Stafford free and the Telephone service is available".

Only a week before the auction the Lusitania had been sunk with the loss of 1,198 lives (785 passengers and 413 crew). The outlook was bleak. Saturday, 15th May, the day of the auction, arrived. There were no bidders and the property was withdrawn. No one was prepared to commit a substantial amount of money to buy the house while such turmoil was going on in Europe.

The estate was eventually sold later in the year, the main house being bought by Mr Osborn, to establish a Preparatory School. The detached house and garden were bought by Mr Rupert Evans, of Evans and Evans, Estate Agents who had been responsible for organising the sale.

Kate Philips

Although the Morton Philips family left the Parish in 1915, they did not forget the Church, sending a generous donation to buy hangings for the sanctuary and a new bible "as one is badly needed".[46]

In due course they also sent a donation towards the costs of the Parish War Memorial. They had lost their son Mark in 1917. News of his death arrived in Staffordshire on 10th October. Morton wrote in his diary, "I was just leaving the office when Kate rang me up - a telegram from the War Office that Mark was killed on the 4th. It is awful - I could not get away tonight.

11th Oct. I got home at 2.30. Kate is crushed, but trying to bear up bravely. We are spared the awful suspense that many have to bear, and we hope and trust that death was instantaneous. That is all for us as yet."

[46] Berkswich Parish Magazine October 1915

68

Chapter 12
Baswich House School

On 31st August, 1915, George Francis Atterbury Osborn, school-master, and his wife Ethelwyn, of "Rydal Mount", Colwyn Bay bought Weeping Cross House from William Morton Philips for £3,250.

It was the intention of the Osborns to create a boys' preparatory school in the building. "Weeping Cross House" now became "Baswich House School". It opened in September 1915 with just three pupils, and never had more than thirty boys on roll at any one time. One pupil to arrive at Baswich House during 1915 was Nevill Francis Mott who went on to win the Nobel Prize for Physics in 1977.

Baswich House Schoolroom

Nevill was born in 1905 in Leeds. His father was Senior Science Master at Giggleswick School and his grandfather was the Arctic explorer, Sir John Richardson. As his father's career developed (eventually he was to become the Chief Education Officer for Liverpool), the family moved to Staffordshire and lived for a time in Brocton. Until he was ten, Nevill was taught at home by his mother, a Cambridge mathematics graduate. Eventually, as Brocton and Cannock Chase became a noisy, busy army camp, instead of a peaceful idyll, it was decided that Nevill should go to a "proper" school.

Although Nevill had nothing but praise for Mr Osborn's teaching of maths, science and Latin, he was not fond of sport, something that was very important within the school. He was not used to mixing with other boys and they called him a "Swot".

He became something of a misfit. At first he was a weekly boarder but the other boys called him names because he was always running home to his parents at weekends.

The boarders slept in small dormitories, which contained four or six iron bedsteads. Each boy had his own chair, dressing table and mirror. Meals were taken in the oak-panelled dining room, the boys sitting on long oak benches either side of four refectory tables. Eventually Nevill became a full boarder and, no doubt, was tormented even more by the other boys as he did not wish to join in the sporting activities which most of them enjoyed in their leisure time. The boys played football, cricket, tennis, table-tennis, learnt to box and exercised regularly on the vaulting horse, horizontal bars and the climbing ropes.

Dormitory at Baswich House

After three years at Baswich House School, Nevill gained a scholarship to Clifton College, Bristol, where he stayed for five years before obtaining a place at Cambridge and embarking on his brilliant career in Physics.

No doubt the Osborns were proud of their pupil's achievements as they continued to prepare other boys for entry into Public School.

On 1st September, 1920 the Osborns threw open the grounds of Baswich House for an "American Tea", which was what we would call a "Bring and Buy". There were many stalls, including garden produce, books, flowers, crafts and a bran tub. The Penkridge "Canaries" gave two concerts in the dining-room and Stafford Borough Military Band played during the afternoon and also in the evening for a "Flannel" Dance[47]. Small girls carried trays of flowers, selling posies and button holes to those present. The event which caused most hilarity was the Men's Beauty

---

[47] We imagine that a Flannel Dance is one where it is not necessary to dress up in a suit. Casual clothes will do.

Competition! Over £50 was raised towards the new heating system in Walton Church!

The Osborns worked hard to establish the school and, during the summer, pupils from other schools would hold camps in the extensive grounds. The picture below has the words "Baswich House Preparatory School - Summer Camp" written on the back. The words "Weeping Cross 1923" are on the cricket bat, and the emblem on one of the girls gym slips seems to show the letters C. L. Where did they come from?

On Thursday morning, 18th November, 1926, Mrs Osborn, who had retired to bed at about 1 a.m. after checking that all was well, was suddenly aware of a strong smell of burning. She awoke her husband who went to investigate. George was beaten back by the smoke and flames as he opened one of the classroom doors. Attempts to put the flames out with a fire extinguisher were useless, and eventually he had to retreat as the smoke and heat became too much. He collapsed as he reached a nearby corridor and had to be helped from the building. The fire brigade, under the command of Chief Fire Officer, Mr A.B. Haywood, arrived within twelve minutes of the alarm being raised. With a plentiful supply of water the blaze was eventually brought under control in just less than two hours.

Mrs Osborn and other members of staff had awoken the twenty eight boarders, told them each to wrap a blanket around themselves, and led them to safety in the school lodge. Mrs Hand, who lived opposite, eventually took charge of several of the boys.

Girls and Staff, Summer Camp 1923

No-one was hurt in the fire but most of their belongings were destroyed. The fire, fanned by a strong east wind, spread rapidly and consumed the classrooms, dormitories, a master's sitting-room and the servants' quarters on the top floor.

Valiant efforts by the fire brigade managed to stop the fire spreading to the main part of the house where Mr & Mrs Osborn lived.

By 1934 Mr Osborn, who was now sixty-two, decided it was time to retire to a quiet spot. He moved to a village called Twyning, just north of Tewkesbury in Gloucestershire.

The sale of the school was put into the hands, once again, of Evans and Evans, Estate Agents of Stafford. One prospective purchaser was James Maurice Browne of Knutsford. His enquiries about the school resulted in a letter from Evans and Evans in April 1934, which said little about the educational establishment but that "The fundamental value of the property lies in its land, which is ripe for immediate development for building and if the land comes on to the market it would sell freely for that purpose.

Morning Break.
The Area in this picture can be seen to the left of the picture on the following page, taken after the fire

In our opinion, the property would realise, if broken up and sold in building plots, the sum of £4,750".[48]

However, Mr Browne was not interested in the building plots, but was keen to develop the school. The sale was eventually completed on 3rd of September 1935, just in time for the new school year.

---

[48] SRO Ref. C 706

After the Fire

The Dining Room

The Gym

Perhaps he did not trust the Osborns, but Maurice insisted that they sign an agreement which stated that "Mr & Mrs Osborn were not to start a school within 100 miles of Baswich House".

Aldwarden Hill, Knutsford

Mr Browne was the son of Mining Engineer, James Tadfil Browne, who became Managing Director of Manchester Collieries Ltd. Prior to the nationalisation of the coal-mining industry the company owned fourteen mines in the Lancashire coalfield.   It would appear that money was no object when this young man of only twenty-nine wished to purchase Baswich House.   The Browne family lived at Aldwarden Hill, Knutsford, an eccentric house built in the Italian style by Richard Harding Watt, a wealthy glove manufacturer, in about 1906.   The house is now a listed building within the Legh Road Conservation Area, Knutsford.

While Maurice's father and brother were both engineers, he followed in his grandparent's, James and Sophie Browne's, footsteps.   They had both been teachers at the National School in Radcliffe-on-Trent, Nottinghamshire.   Teaching was in his blood!

Maurice was educated at Repton where he was Head Boy and Captain of football. He was also very much involved with the Scouting movement. Maurice managed the school alone for three years before he married Betty Jean Harkness in the summer of 1937.   They were married by Dr Geoffrey Fisher, who was, at that time, Bishop of Chester but who would eventually become Archbishop of Canterbury. Dr Fisher had been Headmaster at Repton School during the time Maurice was a pupil.

In 1939 Mr Browne appointed a new member of staff to the school.   Her contract of employment is interesting. Again he puts restrictions on his staff to prevent them working in another school close by, for a period of five years. Not something that would be acceptable today!

Agreement re Appointment,
Baswich House School, 29th July 1939

Nature of Service To Supervise and teach the kindergarten class at Baswich House each day during school terms and piano lessons during hours to be arranged by the employer.

Remuneration £52.0.0 per annum plus one equal third of the fees of each additional pupil the employee shall from time to time have under her charge and certain free meals at Baswich House - provided always that such remunerations shall not exceed £100 per annum.

Duration of Service One term's notice.

Employee

a. To obey orders of the employer and all school regulations

b. To be punctual in discharge of duties

c. To perform same faithfully and to best of ability

d. Not to engage either as principal or employee in any education work including Kindergarten School within 10 miles of Baswich House for a period of 5 years after the termination of present employment without the written consent of the employer.

e. To endeavour to promote the prosperity of the school and in no respect perform any acts or act tending to the damage thereof.

Employer

To provide necessary classrooms, books etc and fires and lights.[49]

By the time this new teacher had taken up her appointment at the start of the autumn term, the world had changed dramatically. On 3rd September 1939, Britain, France, Australia and New Zealand had declared war on Germany.

Maurice Browne, who was still only thirty-four, decided that he was needed in the forces. He joined the Royal Marines and left his wife to run Baswich House School with just a skeleton staff. Mrs Browne found it difficult to manage everything without the support of her husband and it was becoming increasingly difficult to find

James Maurice Browne

---

[49] SRO D1798/684/15/30

and keep staff.   On the 16th July 1940, the Education Office received a short note from a contact, telling them that Mrs Browne would be closing the school at the end of the summer term.[50]   Was this an answer to their prayers?   Perhaps Baswich House could be used as a school for some of the children evacuated from Ramsgate, on the south coast.

James Maurice Browne was invalided out of the services in 1942 after active service in Africa. He taught French at Eton for the remainder of the war years. He died in 1957 aged 51.

When the Kindergarten Department closed at Baswich House the children were taught for a short period in the home of their teacher at Walton and then classes were held in Walton Vicarage at the invitation of the Vicar, Rev. R.N. Lawson.[51]

Gardening at Baswich House School

[50] SRO CEQ/13/4/2
[51] Information from Mr Christopher Philips who was a pupil at Baswich House School for just one year 1939/40

Chapter 13
The War Years

In 1940 nearly 3,500 children were evacuated from Ramsgate to Staffordshire. Stafford was considered to be a safe town and was therefore asked to receive 1,500 of these young people.

In March 1940, the Mayor, Councillor H. Joynes made an appeal to the residents of Stafford to place their names on a Roll of those ready to receive unaccompanied school children who may be sent to the town.

The town responded well and Berkswich was able to accept 400 children into its midst, many of them pupils from Clarendon House Girls' High School.

After negotiations in August 1940 between Staffordshire Education Authority and Evans & Evans, acting as agent for Mr Browne who was now abroad on active service, it was agreed that Baswich House School could be used for accommodation for Clarendon House School, Ramsgate. Under the terms of the agreement, the Education Department had to continue to be responsible for the House and grounds until six months after the end of hostilities.

At first this seemed an ideal solution to housing the Girls' School, but as the Headmistress, Miss Helm, toured the building, she realised that it would not be easy for the school to continue with a full curriculum. There was no gym, no art room and no laboratories.

Clarendon House School, Ramsgate, 2009

A solution was found when Miss Helm and Miss Whitehurst, the Headmistress of Stafford Girls' High School, got together. Miss Helm set out their joint proposals in a letter to the Education Department in August 1940 :-

"Baswich House is to be used by Clarendon House, buildings and grounds for full lessons and games during school hours (9 a.m. - 4 p.m.) on Wednesdays and Fridays for the whole of the middle and lower school. On Mondays I propose a scheme of work, lessons in the more recreative subjects and games, as Monday for us corresponds to Saturday of the High School. Therefore we use the premises 3 full days each week.

Social Purposes. We shall use Baswich House for after school and evening activities so far as can be arranged, probably for girls living near, to alleviate travelling during darkness.

Miss Whitehurst proposes to use Baswich House on Tuesdays and Thursdays while Clarendon House is in possession of the High School.

Baswich House will be in full use five days and probably some evenings" [52]

Stafford Girls' High School

The idea was that for two days a week the girls from Stafford High School would use Baswich House, thus allowing Clarendon House the use of their Laboratories, Gym and Art Room. This solution in itself caused problems, as many of the Stafford High School pupils came to Stafford by train from the surrounding villages such as Gnosall and Stone. The trains were timed to allow them to get to the High School in the Oval, in time for lessons. The extra travelling out of town to Baswich House meant they were often late for lessons. At the end of the day they had to leave early in order to catch the trains that would get them home before dark.

Most of the Clarendon girls were billeted in homes in the south of the town, so travelling was not such a problem. As long as they had a signed letter from their

---

[52] SRO CEQ/13/4/2

parents, these girls would be allowed to cycle to school during the better weather. During the winter, a bus was provided for those who lived too far away to walk.

The Chief Education Officer for Kent was responsible for the running costs of Baswich House. It is surprising how small, by today's standards, this amount was. Rent £310 p.a., Rates, £98.10s 0d, fuel & light £100, Caretaker and upkeep of Playing Fields £117, making a grand total of £625 10s 0d. (£625 50p)

The Education Department in Kent had another problem to solve. So many children had been evacuated to Staffordshire from various parts of the country, there was a shortage of desks and chairs! Baswich House Preparatory School had at most, only 30 pupils, and therefore only 30 desks and chairs. It was proposed to bring 290 girls from Kent! Eventually, 141 folding desks were sent to Stafford from Kent, but they had no chairs! Once these domestic matters were solved, the girls moved in. Clarendon House School was in residence at Baswich House on Monday, Wednesday and Friday, while Stafford High School had possession on Tuesday and Thursday.

Miss Helm noted that the cellars at Baswich House had three exits and would, in the event of an air raid, hold up to 100 girls[53]. Further shelters would be necessary in the grounds if all the girls were to be safe. They were some time in coming and, as a result, at the sound of the siren, the girls who could not squeeze into the cellars would crouch under their desks until the "All-Clear" sounded!

All was not perfect. Rats were a common problem in the house and a contract worth 30/- (£1 50p) for their destruction was renewed every year while the girls were in residence!

Mr Capewell was the Caretaker. Originally he had been responsible for the upkeep of the grounds but, as more people enlisted in the armed forces or were involved in war work, he was expected to care for the house as well. He had some help in 1941 when Mrs Williams moved into a bed-sit in one of the attic rooms in return for supervising the cleaning of the house and helping with fire watching. Her assistance, she hoped, would give Mr Capewell more time in the evenings.

Miss Helm was, however, unhappy about the standard of work undertaken by Capewell and there appears to have been quite a battle going on between the Head and the Caretaker.

In an attempt to help the war effort, the girls were encouraged to grow vegetables - Miss Helm made it quite clear that Mr Capewell would not be involved in this venture in any way whatsoever! Mr Hall, who lived in one of the cottages in the grounds, requested permission to build a chicken run and keep a few hens. Approval was given.

Joan Tyldesley was a pupil at Stafford Girls' High School in 1940. She recalls fondly the times she spent in Baswich House. "I remember the excitement of entering this lovely rambling old building with its dull red bricks and little casement windows with pointed eves. I remember the brass knobs fixed to the bannisters on each stairway to prevent sliding! We thought the authorities were real spoil sports! We attended Baswich House for just two days per week and sometimes found little

---

[53] In 2009, just before demolition, members of Berkswich History Society photographed the cellar. It was very small and only had one exit. It would appear that part of the cellar must have been filled in some time after the war.

notes in our desks thanking us for sharing. Eventually I met my desk sharer and we became friends.

Being war-time of course there was little or no heating in the winter months, but everyone accepted the situation. We all arrived at Baswich House armed with rugs, gloves or mittens, scarves, boots, heavy coats and hot water bottles which we were allowed to refill from time to time. We kept them pressed to our tummies wrapped in rugs!

There were stories going round that the place was haunted, which added to the excitement.

I lived on the Cannock Road so it was an easy walk for me. I used to go through the little wooden gate in the fence just by "Green Shutters", the first house in Cannock Road. There was a mysterious manhole cover in the grass as one entered this gate. We used to invent tales of it being a hide out for German spies!"

Muriel Lightfoot was also a student at the Stafford High School in 1940. She recalls how, on the day the evacuees arrived in Stafford from Ramsgate, the High School closed for the day.

"On Mondays and Wednesdays each girl had to meticulously pack her leather satchel with all the text and exercise books required for the following day, plus their evening homework books as these would all be needed the next day at Baswich House. Assembly was held every morning in one of the oak panelled rooms on the ground floor. The classrooms were mainly on the first floor but some lessons were held on the second floor which meant climbing the narrow staircase used in earlier years by the servants."

One parent was concerned for the safety of the girls. A letter in the Parish Magazine reads - "May I, as a parent and guardian of evacuated children utter a word of caution to other parents and guardians regarding a local tendency on the part of some of our girls to strike up friendships with prisoners of war stationed here to work on the land.

Anderson Shelter

Such friendships are very unwise from many points of view and in some parts of the country have landed girls in very serious trouble for infringing regulations. Parents and guardians would be well advised to have a talk with the older girls pointing out the dangers and warning them to avoid contacts - however innocently begun - that may end in disaster" No doubt the two single lady headmistresses would see that their girls obeyed the rules!

In November 1940, the War Department requested the use of three rooms on the first floor of Baswich House for the period of hostilities at a yearly rent of one peppercorn.

Percy Smith remembers events during the War when he was a Fire Watcher. "The Fire Watchers were based at Baswich House, where they assembled in an Anderson Shelter. This was a dug out 6' 6" x 6', entered by concrete steps. It had a semi-circular corrugated iron roof that had turf over it. The door was of cleated corrugated iron to make it fairly air-tight. There were a few holes drilled in the door and there was a ventilator up through the turf. It was very cold in the shelter and there was not much room to move. The watchers gathered at the shelter as quickly as possible if the Stafford sirens sounded. This was usually when enemy aircraft had been spotted coming towards the coast. The firewatchers were then on duty all night until the "All- Clear" sounded.

The watchers' job was to douse any flares that might be dropped by enemy reconnaissance planes to guide the bomber pilots to a target. To this end, they were supplied with canvas buckets which stood up when full of water and packed flat when empty. They each held at least two gallons and were therefore very heavy to carry.

Smith Gun

Fire Watchers collaborated with the ARP Wardens, whose job it was to deal with incendiaries. They were trained to evacuate an area should a bomb be dropped and to cope with all eventualities. They had to check that a total blackout was observed. Every building had to have thick, black curtains behind ordinary curtains or lightweight wooden frames covered in thick black fabric which were held in place by "turn buttons". ARP Wardens wore a dark uniform of thickly-woven, fire-retardant material with "ARP" buttons and "ARP" embroidered high on the left side of the chest. They wore tin[54] helmets.

The Fire Watchers at Baswich House included Bert Oakley who was a reserve policeman, George Brearly from Cannock Road, who was a traveller for Heinz Foods and if he was away on business, his wife Kath, stood in for him and Margaret Rooker, who lived at Green Shutters, the first house on Cannock Road past Baswich House."

---

[54] "Tin" helmets were actually made of steel.

Towards the end of 1943, the Home Guard requested permission to use the garage, which had the Music Room over it, to store Smith Guns and trailers. No thought of Health & Safety then. It was agreed that the guns could be stored as long as the Home Guard was responsible for their safe custody, for locking up the premises and for any damage they did!

Henry Teasdale remembers his father, Edward Grosvenor Teasdale, becoming a major in the Home Guard where he commanded "B" Company in Stafford, under the battalion commander, Lieutenant Colonel Fisher, who was Biology master at King Edward VI Grammar School. Henry recalls an occasion, when as a boy of about 10, he was asked to meet his father at Baswich House which was then Company H.Q. As he walked up the drive, a Wolseley saloon car pulled up along side him and offered him a lift. Henry could not believe his luck, it was a rare privilege to be able to run a civilian car during the war years and an even rarer treat for a small boy to get a ride in one. The driver was Lord Lichfield, (Thomas Edward Anson, 4th Earl) who was second-in-command to Mr Teasdale. Henry was told to hop on to the running board and hang on to the near-side door handle. He felt rather like a footman to his Lordship, whom he recalls as a rather shy, white-haired gentleman who didn't want to be burdened with high office.

In 1944, the House was used each Wednesday and Thursday during February and March for Fire Guard Training. However, Mr Capewell saw this as an opportunity to make money. He informed Major Mackenzie (Civil Defence) that he was in the habit of receiving 2/6 (12.5 p) from the Wardens and Fire Guards to compensate him for his extra hours of work!

In May 1944, Mr Browne returned to Stafford on leave. He was somewhat shocked to find that the buildings and the grounds had deteriorated dramatically since he gave permission for his school to be used by the Education Authority. He stated that everything was in excellent order when he handed it over.

Mr Browne had had enough. Baswich House was to be sold by auction once again. Because of the "serious condition of neglect", Mr Capewell continued for the time being, in his job as full-time caretaker-gardener, living in the Lodge.

Clarendon House School remained in Stafford until Christmas 1944. After four and a half years in the town the girls and staff were genuinely sad when the time came to leave. At the breaking up ceremony, Miss Helm spoke warmly of the hospitality of the people of Stafford. In his reply, the mayor, Mr H. Wallace-Copeland commented on the good behaviour of the pupils and the high reputation of the school. As a final act Miss Helm wrote personal letters to thank everyone who had received one of "her girls" into their homes.

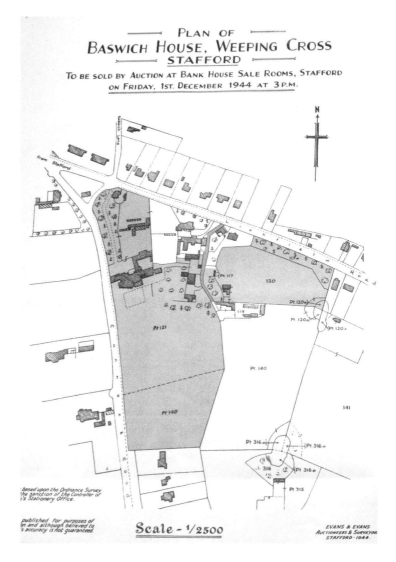

Plan of the Property as depicted in "Schedule for Sale" in 1944

117a	Spinney	120	Football Field
Pt 121	House & Garden	Pt 117	Shrubbery
Pt 140	Cricket Field		

Chapter 14
1945 – 1952

Once again estate agents Evans & Evans were responsible for the sale. The Auction was held at 3.00 p.m. on 1st December, 1944 at their sale rooms in Stafford. The estate was bought by John Joules & Sons, Brewers of Stone for £6,750. The formalities were completed and Baswich House conveyed to the Brewery on 4th April, 1945. They intended turning the building into an hotel. It was clear that the war was nearly at an end but Joules knew that it would be some time before the government would allow building work to go ahead on luxuries such as hotels. The priority would be to build factories and thousands of houses for returning servicemen and their families.

With a desperate shortage of housing, Stafford Town Council approached John Joules to see if Baswich House could be used, on a short term lease, as accommodation for some of their staff. The Brewery was only too happy with the suggestion and the building was converted into nine flats. The three cottages in the grounds were already let: Lodge Cottage at a rent of 10/- per week to George Bradbury, Garden Cottage at a rent of 6/4d per week to Mr Tunnicliffe and the third cottage to Charles Hall at £2 per annum!

In 1948, one of the second floor flats was occupied by the Stocker family. William worked for Stafford Town Council while Mum stayed at home to care for the two girls who were aged six and four and a half. The flat was spacious and the best room, although it had probably only been used by the staff in the past, was half panelled. Because the panelling made it dark and dreary, the room was not used that often. However, under the window seat was a wonderful cupboard for playing hide and seek. The girls had freedom to run up and down the long corridor during the day but, once the occupiers of the flat below (other employees of the Town Council) returned from work, they had to be quiet. The girls spent many happy hours exploring the grounds looking for birds eggs and wild flowers. Although only young, they travelled to St Leonard's School on the bus by themselves. If the weather was fine they would often walk home alone - a journey of over a mile - along a main road.

The Stocker Family

It was always a drag to take the washing down two flights of stairs to hang it outside and then to run down again to fetch it in when dry. It was even more annoying having to dash down stairs when it suddenly started raining. This problem was solved by the discovery of a flat roof which could be reached by climbing out of the kitchen window. A clothes line fixed to the wall was long enough to dry two sheets at a time and saved endless trips up and down stairs. The Stockers were not the first people to make use of this area. An old parasol was found tucked away on the roof.

Someone, perhaps one of the servants from a previous era or one of the staff when the house was used as a school, had found a very private place for a spot of sunbathing.

The walled kitchen garden still remained, and each flat had a portion in which to grow flowers and vegetables. Many foods were still rationed and it was a great help to be able to "grow your own".

Stafford Borough Council Cricket Team at Baswich House, 1949

Baswich House became the home ground for the Borough Council Cricket Team for the period that the Council leased the house. The adult committee of Walton Youth Club obtained permission for members of the Club to use the football field, and Weeping Cross Tennis Club continued to play on the two courts close to Baswich House.

On 18th February 1950 the Stafford "Newsletter" carried the following. "Plans to convert a block of flats into a luxury hotel were outlined at Stafford Borough Licensing Justices Annual Meeting on Monday. Application was made for the sale of intoxicants at Baswich House, Weeping Cross, Stafford.

Making application on behalf of John Joules, Kenneth Mynett said there was a lack of accommodation for people visiting Stafford and it was well known that visitors to Stafford had to travel as far away as Stone and Rugeley to obtain accommodation."

Among facilities at the proposed hotel would be tennis courts, a bowling green, and ten acres of gardens. A bar, two smoke rooms, lounge and dining room were planned for the ground floor with bedrooms on the first and second floors. Three of the bedrooms would have private bathrooms. There would also be a private dining room and residents' lounge on the first floor, reached by a lift and separate staircase. The furniture and fittings would be of the best, and the hotel would be a definite "asset" to the town of which Stafford could be proud. It was further argued that there were no other licensed premises situated within ¼ mile of the site. The English Electric Company, which was expanding, would find it convenient to accommodate its overseas visiting representatives. Alderman Bostock, who supported the application, said there was a need for further and better accommodation in the town. In addition the population of Stafford was moving towards Baswich and another hotel was not only desirable but necessary. If plans for the hotel were approved, Messrs Joules would surrender their Full Licence of the Lamb Inn in Broad Eye, Stafford. The Chairman of the Licensing Justices, Alderman George Owen said that the Justices approved of the plans and the application would be granted subject to the approval of the confirming authority.

The Lamb Inn, Broad Eye

In August 1950 the lease expired, and an undertaking was given by the Town Clerk that vacant possession would be given to the Brewery and the tenants found alternative accommodation. It was, however, made clear to the Brewery that "The baths and other fittings installed by the Stafford Corporation remain the property of the Corporation and may be removed by the Corporation!"

The plans to convert Baswich House into an hotel did not come to fruition and the "proposed" alterations were never started as the Ministry of Works refused to grant a licence for the work.

Chapter 15
The Police Take Over

In 1952 Baswich House and its grounds were acquired for £8,260.[55] by Staffordshire County Council for use by Staffordshire County Police as a Motor Training Centre. The only buildings on the site at this time were the main house, the stable block, and three small bungalows

Baswich House was first occupied by the Police on 1st April 1954. Prior to this, the Motor Training Centre was based at Seighford Hall, (four miles north of Stafford). In 1954, it was Force Policy that only suitably qualified drivers would be authorised to drive police vehicles. In order to qualify, potential drivers were required to attend one or more of the Standard, Intermediate or Advanced driving courses. These courses were of four or five week duration, and students were expected to live in accommodation provided at Baswich House. Later the Training Centre's activities were further expanded to cover Motor Cycles, Heavy Goods Vehicles, and Buses.

Baswich House was also used as accommodation for Police Cadets, who attended a two week Residential Course after joining the Force. Meals were taken together in the oak-panelled dining room of the house. Students were required to stand until the arrival of the Senior Officer who would say "grace". The kitchen garden within the grounds provided many of the vegetables for these meals.

Trevor Houlton recalls his time at the Training Centre. "In the early 1970's I returned to Baswich House for driver training. Panda cars had been introduced in 1967, and stations went from having just one car, mainly for use by the Inspector or Sergeant, to cars for everyone! Suddenly every police officer needed to be able to drive police cars. As a stopgap one of the Instructors from Baswich House would travel from station to station and spend an hour being driven around by each officer. If he felt you would not be a danger to others, he issued a permit! The rest were allocated a driving course at Stafford. I was fortunate and, for five years, escaped the dreaded training. Eventually the net closed in and I was enlisted on the Standard 5 week driving course at Baswich House."

The Driving School not only catered for Staffordshire students. Tt became a Home Office approved Driving Centre and took in students from adjoining Forces, (e.g. Stoke City, Wolverhampton Borough, Walsall and Dudley Boroughs,) together with nearby County Forces. In addition, many overseas students attended and qualified. All the Driving Instructors were serving Police Officers.

Baswich House was a hive of activity with large numbers of officers sleeping in the upstairs rooms over the classrooms. The main classroom was right at the end of the building, nearest to Cannock Road. Along the corridor were several smaller rooms, which were offices for the instructors. It was a highly disciplined environment. When the Sergeant or Inspector entered a classroom, everyone stood to attention.

---

[55] Staffordshire Advertiser 23 Nov 1961

Police Cars at Baswich House, 1963

There were three groups of trainees. The Standard Driving Course lasted 5 weeks and concluded with the usual test drive, which was slightly unfair on those who had never driven before. Trevor Houlton goes on to say, "I was one of the lucky ones with plenty of experience, but I was shocked at the amount we had to learn. Each morning a couple of trainees would be asked to stand and recite long paragraphs from the Driving Manual before being told to "board cars" which were parked outside Baswich House. We each stood by one of the car doors and only on the command opened the door and sat in. Another order was barked out and we all slammed the doors in unison. Speed limits, apart from the 30 mph one were ignored and on my test travelling up Yarlet Bank at 100 mph I told the instructor a Rolls Royce was following close behind. The instructor turned right round and stared at the driver who braked and then vanished.

The Intermediate Course lasted 4 weeks and was intended to put more types of vehicles onto your driving permit. Panda cars (Austin 1100's) were the only vehicles Standard Course drivers could use. The Intermediate Course taught drivers to use people carriers and the crime cars (Ford Cortinas).

Finally the Advanced Course was four weeks of total concentration. At least three cars, mainly Jaguars (both manual and automatic), would leave Baswich House at 9 a.m. and head for destinations such as Devizes in Wiltshire. The Wiltshire police would arrange for us to eat at their Headquarters and we raced to be first. Driver change-overs took place at traffic lights when on red! If we were fortunate to beat the others, the instructor would tell us to sit really composed as if we had been in Devizes for at least half an hour before the others arrived!

Morning Parade

One trip finished with an Austin 1800 on a motorway hard shoulder with smoke coming from the engine! In the tradition of helping one another we picked up two occupants of this car and I spent the next 70 miles sitting in front of our Jaguar, on top of the handbrake.

Unfortunately, my Advanced Course ended in tragedy. It was the early 1970's and, after our celebration meal, three advanced drivers went in their own car along the Cannock Road intending to go to a night club in Cannock. They did not get to Cannock. All three were killed in a crash close to the Seven Stars Public House just over a mile from Baswich House. A stolen car had been travelling on the wrong side of the road and ran into them. The next day the atmosphere was terrible. We all stood in front of Baswich House beside our cars in almost total silence for the rest of the day."

Joy Lewis also recalls her memories of Baswich House. "I left school in June 1969, aged 17 years; my father was a police officer and, having been brought up in that environment, I decided that I should like to work for the Police, but as a civilian. I had a successful interview at Police Headquarters, Stafford, for a secretarial job at the Motor Training Centre, Baswich House. When I started work my boss, the Senior Instructor, was Inspector Ronald Biggs. He told me that he was looking for a young person that he could train. He was a wonderful man, a good teacher, and he taught me such a lot about good office practice. The Great Train Robbery had happened just a few years before and two of the gang members were Ronald Biggs and Bruce

Reynolds. My maiden name was Reynolds and my boss was of course Ronald Biggs. We used to get teased by people saying "a couple of criminals work in there – Biggs and Reynolds."

Baswich House was a really lovely building in which to work; the top floors housed the bedrooms for the students attending courses, whilst the bottom floor housed the senior instructors and my office, a large room for the car instructors and a smaller one for the motorcycle instructors. There was an exhibits room where students learned about car maintenance, a classroom for car students and a classroom for motorcycle students.

I was a young woman working with a number of fun-loving male car and motorcycle instructors who all helped me and treated me with the greatest respect. After some time Inspector Biggs was promoted and moved to another Division. My new boss was Inspector Lewis Brindley and we got on very well from the start. He was most proficient at his job and had an unusual sense of humour.

After ten years I left the Motor Training Centre and Baswich House to have my first child. By then I had a new boss - Chief Inspector Brian Coker, a very caring and thoughtful man. Whilst I was expecting he made sure everything was to hand and that I did not need to stretch or bend over. Sadly Brian died recently.

Driving & Motor Cycle Instructors with Mrs Joy Lewis outside Baswich House, 1979

I still encounter some of the motorcycle instructors as my husband, Alan, keeps in touch with the OPBs (Old Police Bikers), with whom we have occasional meetings at a local pub or a "bike run out" in the summer. I will always remember my ten wonderful years at Baswich House."

In July, 1961 the Force Mounted Section moved up from Eastgate Street, Stafford, to the Baswich House site, which was now the "County Police Headquarters". The Mounted Branch had been housed in stables at the rear of what is now the County Treasurer's Department, and close to the present County Record Office at the rear of the William Salt Library. The new accommodation consisted of the old stable block in the grounds of Baswich House, together with a modern extension. At one time, fifteen working police horses were stabled on the site.

The history of the Mounted Branch goes back to 1894 when twelve saddles and harnesses were purchased for use on horses hired for special occasions and events, and 12 officers were nominated to be riders. In 1919, after the Great War, a permanent Mounted Branch was established with horses returned from the battlefields of Europe. Mounted Branch officers pre-fixed their collar numbers with the letter 'M'. All horses were given names beginning with the letter 'S'. The horses were a regular sight in the area, often exercising on nearby Cannock Chase. After 81 years distinguished service to the force, the Mounted Branch was disbanded in April 2000.

Stables at Baswich House demolished circa 2002

In 1955 the then Chief Constable, Colonel George Hearn, C.B.E., decided that it would be appropriate to form a Dog Branch. The first three Constables at Baswich to be allocated dogs were P.C.'s Howell, Beckley and Grass.

A special Dog Branch block was built adjacent to the stables and training was done at Baswich House. The main training was of course, done outside the Headquarters, but discipline tests were undertaken on the front lawn. Many local people remember that the dogs undertook their training with military precision on the lawn where they could be clearly seen working with their handlers. With the success that followed, Baswich House eventually became a Regional Training Centre for dogs with handlers attending from many other Police Forces in the UK and abroad. Not only Police dogs, but also dogs used by HM Forces, Ministry of Defence and Prison Service were trained. It was during this period that dogs were being utilised more and more by law enforcement agencies. In May 1970, at least 24 kennels, together with a small animal surgery, were built to house dogs attending these courses.

PC Tim Nicklin on Santon

Sgt. Gurt Muller and his Dog

The few historic items and artifacts which the force owned were, for many years, kept under the stewardship of D.C. John Harris. It had always been the responsibility of the Crime Prevention Department, as it was then known, to look after these treasures. Few knew of their content or location. They were stored in the cellar of the Stores Block. Sadly in the mid 1960's the cellar was very badly flooded and several items were destroyed. Those items which were left were retrieved and placed in a more suitable storage area. Only on very rare occasions were any of these displayed.

Horses and staff at Baswich House 1998

In 1976 Mr. Charles Kelly, C.B.E., K.St.J., Q.P.M., D.L., LL.B., was transferred from Essex Police on promotion to Deputy Chief Constable of Staffordshire. That was the start of a long and distinguished time in Staffordshire by a very caring man, who was and still is, passionate about the County as a whole. He was appointed Chief Constable to the Force in July 1977. Fortunately he was also passionate about the history of the Staffordshire Force, having a keen interest in local history and, in particular, military history during the First World War. He felt it only right that we should be proud of our historic roots, and officers who were part of the force should know and be proud of their heritage. It was as a direct result of his passion that the Staffordshire Police Museum was established in 1992 partly to herald the 150th Anniversary of the Force.

Charles Kelly admires his "Peeler" statue

The museum was officially opened by the Chief Constable and his wife, Mrs Doris Kelly and they were presented with a small statue of an 1880's "Peeler". The inscription reads "Presented to C.H. Kelly Chief Constable on the occasion of the official opening of the Staffordshire Police Museum 10th July 1993. The sculptors were Richard & Valerie Green of Bournemouth.

P.C. Alan Lewis was the first police officer to start on the museum project, and a small Committee was established to coordinate the effort. This included the Chief Constable as Chairman, Superintendent John Davis - a local man who worked at that time at Headquarters, Inspector David Baldwin - a true lover of police history matters, Sergeant Alan Walker who acted as Secretary, and P.C. Alan Lewis. Also on the Committee were retired police officers Harvey Birch, Rex Dinsdale and Frank Cadwallader. The latter two had first-hand experience of matters relating to the north of the County. Also co-opted onto the committee was a local lady who proved most valuable - Mrs. Brenda Cardwell. Retired Sergeant Vic Turton also did much work in formulating the Personnel Registers which contained the details of every man and woman who entered the force. As a result he was later co-opted onto the Committee. All Committee members spent many hours in Baswich House maintaining and recording all the historic records and artifacts. They all worked in their own time to create a museum which was a pride and joy to be involved in. At the height of its popularity, over 5,500 people attended the museum in a year. In addition, in order to make it meaningful and provide up to date information, it was normal that the visitors be shown around the Information Room. This was all out of duty time and always so much appreciated by visitors.

In 1995 a large group of men and women who were evacuated to Stafford from Kent during the 2nd World War visited the House. There was much excitement, and a few tears too, on that occasion. Baswich House was, after all, like home to them for a time.

The Police Museum on Opening Day

In about the year 2000 the Government started 'Heritage Weekends' where local historic houses and museums are open free of charge to visitors on a particular weekend. It is fair to say that local people flocked to Baswich House to look inside and see the museum collection. Baswich House itself always remained a real favourite. The Museum grew rapidly in size and reputation. It became an Associate Member of the Museums Commission and was hoping to achieve Registration, a tough standard for any museum. The Committee had a lot of help from Chris Copp, Senior Museums Officer of the Staffordshire County Council. An application for Lottery Funding was made, for improving the state of the building, and after a great deal of hard work was successful. Several hundreds of thousands of pounds were offered on one condition, that the Museum had a lease of at least 20 years. Sadly Chief Constable John Giffard refused to grant such a lease and declined to give any reason for his decision.

The house was "let go" and no or very little maintenance work was undertaken. As with all buildings, the ravages of weather and lack of use soon took their toll and eventually damp took over. Plaster began to fall off walls, windows were broken and went unrepaired and the house which was generally uncared for, slowly began to deteriorate. For all involved in the museum, it was so hard to witness.

The Committee realised at an early stage that they would have to try and find a new home for the collection. The Chief Constable, John Giffard, did try and find suitable premises but without success. David Baldwin and Alan Walker both fought hard to save the collection from being split, again to no avail. The whole of the collection does still remain in the County of Staffordshire and we must be forever thankful to the County Archivist, Thea Randall, for the assistance she gave in saving all the documents and books from the collection. We remain hopeful that the public will be able to access the archives whenever required.[56]

Open Day, 1996

---

[56] In 2009 some items that had been sent to Stoke on Trent Museum had still not been "unwrapped".

Baswich House was a wonderful home for the historic items associated with the Force. All sorts of ideas were broached in order to try to save the building but again to no avail. The site was more valuable with the museum disbanded and out of the building. The museum "staff" were the last people to leave the house in 2007. There was bitter sadness when the items were taken away to various corners of the County and the museums lovely old home destroyed.

Under the leadership of Chief Constable Charles Kelly, Baswich House was annually the centre of a great community event. Police Headquarters was thrown open to the public, usually on a Saturday in July. There was a small charge for a programme, the proceeds of which made a considerable sum for the Force Welfare Fund. There were tours of the Stables and the Control Room and the dogs and horses put on displays. The horses always proved a very popular draw and were loved by all. Their riders were not only dedicated police men and women but also devoted to their horses. Children were allowed to explore the inside of a police car and roundabouts and rides were installed for the benefit of many youngsters. Hundreds of people attended this event each year. This was a great public relations exercise as also was the S.P.A.C.E. programme (Staffordshire Police Activity & Community Enterprise) where the police were involved with organising outdoor

activities for young people during the long summer holidays. The S.P.A.C.E. programme had a noticeable impact on juvenile crime during the month of August. The scheme was started in 1981 and ten years later was catering for 25,000 children and young persons each summer.

The "Open Days" ceased when Charles Kelly retired as Chief Constable.

Gone are the dogs, the horses, the museum and the community involvement of the present day Police Force.

.

Shield to mark the "S.P.A.C.E." Programme

Chapter 16

Planning Matters

In 1998 there was a need for extra office space at Police Headquarters, so the Police Authority commissioned a Feasibility Study to see if additional accommodation could be provided within Baswich House. P.H. Courtis who was, at that time, Property Consultant to the Police Authority, undertook the survey. Although some work was necessary it was reported, "From the preliminary visual inspection it appears that the structure of the building is generally in good condition".

Even with all these offices plus Baswich House and Crossfields House, on the opposite side of Cannock Road, more room was required

Three rooms on the second floor required floor strengthening to bring their load bearing capacity up to office standard and be able to support heavy office equipment.

There was no fire escape from the second floor which was the main reason for this particular area of the building being used only for storage. The roof was considered good with only one small leak, the external brickwork was generally in good order, and the second floor level was safe to walk on.

There was no suggestion in this report that the building was unsafe or in a dangerous state. In the light of events yet to come, it is clear that this is not what the Police Authority wanted to hear.

Nothing further happened that we know of, until 16th March 2001 when a male employee working within Baswich House had an accident. He fell and was injured whilst in the process of moving equipment boxes in the corridor adjacent to the Technical Support Unit store on the ground floor, or that is the official version. One unofficial and unconfirmed story is that he fell over a TV/Computer Monitor that had been in the corridor for some days, waiting to be moved! Whatever the reason, the air ambulance was called and the patient was taken to hospital where he remained for several days as a result of injuries to his back and neck.

The Health & Safety Executive now became involved. If an employee is away from work for more than 3 days as a result of an accident at work, it is necessary for the employer to report it. The Inspector of Health and Safety was concerned about various aspects of the working practices in parts of Baswich House. However, nothing was actually said about the state or condition of the building itself. The then Chief Constable, John Giffard, answered these concerns by volunteering the information, without any pressure from the Health & Safety Executive, that all staff would be relocated from Baswich House by the end of 2001.

When the demolition of Baswich House became imminent early in 2009, letters were exchanged with the Chief Executive of the Police Authority, Mr Alan Wallis, regarding the closure of the building. In a letter dated 25th February, 2009, Mr Wallis stated, "The fire alarm has not been operated or maintained since Baswich House was vacated in March 2001: the power supply to the building was disconnected from this date".

How strange then that the Police Museum Visitors Book, which is now deposited in the County Record Office, contains the following dated entries -

1st March, 2002 - David Kidney, M.P., "Such history, such memories, a truly valuable resource".

13th March 2003. Two ladies from Ramsgate, J.M. & V.J. "Evacuees to Stafford for five years throughout the war. Went to school in Baswich House. Lovely to return from Ramsgate".

2nd November 2004. Visit to museum by 8 members of the Police Committee, including the Chairman, Michael Poulter, and Vice-Chairman, David Pearsall.[57]

Volunteers also stated that they continued to help at the Museum after March 2001.

Was the building really vacated in March 2001? Or was the Police Museum operating without electricity or fire/burglar alarm protection for the last years of its existence? Draw your own conclusions!

On the 1st August 2003, Gough Planning Services, now the Police Authority's Planning Consultants, submitted a six-page document to the Borough Council to accompany a planning application to develop land around Baswich House for housing.

Police Houses earmarked for demolition. Baswich House can be seen in the background

---

[57] SRO C/PC/12/19/3/1

The document made two interesting comments. First, "Although Baswich House is not listed, it is recognised that this building may be worthy of retention," and secondly "With the exception of Baswich House, most of the structures presently on the site will be demolished and replaced with new dwelling houses". Four possible layouts submitted with the planning application all showed Baswich House retained and converted into apartments. It appears that in August 2003, there was no intention to demolish Baswich House.

On 6th August the application was returned to Gough Planning Services, together with a planning fee cheque for £5,500, as the application was incomplete.

After correction, the planning application was eventually received and accepted as valid on 22nd September 2003. Stafford Borough Council Planning Department immediately wrote letters to all residents living around the site asking for their comments. Letters were also sent to such organisations as Severn Trent Water, the Highways Agency, Staffordshire Education Department and many other public bodies that could be affected by the development. The recipients had twenty-one days in which to reply.

The general response from local residents was that the development proposals would result in even more traffic on already busy roads. The Education Authority requested a contribution of £153,462 towards providing the extra places that would be required at Walton High School should the development go ahead. Concern was such that, on 8th October 2003, John Francis, Borough Councillor for the Weeping Cross area, asked that the application be "Called In". His action meant that the decision on the planning application would be taken by the full planning committee and not delegated to officers.

Over the following weeks letters passed from the Borough Planning Department to Gough Planning trying to elicit information from the Police Authority. On the 29th January 2004 a memo came from Police HQ to the Planning Office "I have been chasing the application. I have and am continuing to chase our consultants in providing a response for your committee. I know you mentioned an initial deadline of a committee on the 4th February but you also suggested that if this was not the case then it would/could go to your later date in February. I am not sure at this moment how much information I will be able to get from our consultants so if the latter date is possible this may help".

In fact, it was already too late. Planning authorities must either reach a decision within 8 weeks or agree an extension of time with the applicant. The Borough Council did neither and by 29th January it was already more than 18 weeks since the initial application. This meant that the Borough lost the power to determine the application and impose conditions which might have protected Baswich House.

Meanwhile, the Police Authority's right hand did not appear to know what its left hand was doing since, on the 12th January, 2004, Gough Planning had already submitted appeal documents to the Planning Inspectorate in Birmingham, "In respect of the failure of Stafford Borough Council to determine Planning Application Reference 03/00999/OUT to provide housing on land at Police Headquarters, Cannock Road, Stafford."

Given the failings of the Borough, the Police Authority had two choices – either they had to appeal or to withdraw their application and re-submit it. One might have expected public authorities to co-operate on an issue involving a major development which would have an impact, not just on immediate neighbours, but on the whole area - but this was not to be. Perhaps the Police Authority gambled that they would get a more favourable response from a Planning Inspector than they would by giving Stafford Borough a second chance. However, an appeal involved more delay and it would not be until 1st September that the Inspector would hear their case.

Again there was frustration from Borough Council Officers. In July 2004, one senior officer was "concerned over the lack of co-operation which the Council (SBC) has received from the appellant (SPA) with this application. It would therefore appear that the Council is being blocked from progressing this matter due to lack of communication and the intransigence of the appellant".

As the Appeal date approached, the Chief Constable, John Giffard, briefed Mr John Hobson, Q.C. from Gray's Inn, a leading expert in planning law, to represent the Police Authority. It is in a letter to Mr Hobson that the first indication that Baswich House may have to be demolished appears. "It is also probable that in the interim period Baswich House and some of the houses would remain vacant, and as there is no potential for future reuse by the force, consideration would need to be given to their demolition. Should this not prove possible the future maintenance would create an additional financial burden upon the force".

It is interesting to note that the Chief Constable makes no reference to any alleged unsafe state of Baswich House or the accident, which occurred in 2001!

The ins and outs of the planning application and the appeal are complex. All the relevant documents cover several hundred pages and do not make interesting reading for those of us who do not have planning knowledge. The main concern of local residents was with what was to become of Baswich House!

In his Appeal Decision dated 27th September, 2004, the Inspector, Mr A.D. Robinson allowed the Appeal in favour of Staffordshire Police Authority, but made the following comment regarding procedural matters. "I note that the application does not include any proposals for Baswich House. No decision has yet been made as to whether the building is to be retained and converted to residential use or whether it is to be demolished and the site used for the erection of new residential units. Whatever decision is taken as to the future of the building, this is to be the subject of a separate application."

Unfortunately, this overlooked the fact that demolition did not require planning permission, simply service of notice of intention to demolish.

Within his formal decision the Inspector also stated "That no development shall take place until a detailed bat survey has been carried out within all buildings and trees on the site".

As the Planning Inspector had now indicated that it would be necessary for a separate planning application to be submitted before any work was undertaken on Baswich House, everyone breathed a sigh of relief, but not for long.

Rumours were rife within the confines of Police Headquarters. No maintenance work had been done on the building for several years and gossip suggested that Baswich House would be demolished without any reference to the Planning Authority. Once it was destroyed no-one could do anything about it!

The concerns of local residents resulted in an application being made to have the building listed by the Secretary of State for Culture, Media and Sport in conjunction with English Heritage.

The Stafford Borough Council Conservation Officer visited Baswich House with the English Heritage Inspector. "From her brief inspection, the Conservation Officer considers that there is no immediate danger of disrepair or loss: she could see no evidence of any existing structural problems and it seemed quite weather tight. The option of adaptive re-use would therefore appear to remain a viable option." [58]

If the application to list the building was successful there would be no chance of it being demolished. This would restrict the use of the land and the number of houses, which could be built on the site. In April 2007 the Police Member/Officer Working Group of the Police Authority was told, "should the building be given listed status it is envisaged the overall market value of the site to be disposed of would be affected. The marketing exercise is due to begin in September 2007". The only Police Authority Members recorded as being present at this meeting were the Chairman, Michael Poulter and his Deputy, David Pearsall.

During October, The Police Authority continued with their plans to move from Weeping Cross to premises at Lanchester Court, close to the Weston Road Police Vehicle Maintenance site. The move would be costly, and would involve conversion of the existing site into a central amenities block with a reception area and conference facilities. The sale of land at Headquarters was important. The proceeds from the deal would help fund the move and the necessary "improvements".

On 23rd October 2007, English Heritage decided that Baswich House should not be designated as a listed building, citing three main reasons. Firstly it was a fairly typical example of Tudor Revival architecture and it was not particularly distinguished. Secondly, although some features of note remained, much of the interior had been stripped. Finally, the original

Linen Fold Door in Baswich House Dining Room

---

[58] Letter from Stafford Borough Council to David Kidney, M.P. 5th April 2007.

design has been compromised externally by the addition of a large mid 20th century extension to the east.[59] While local residents were devastated at the news, the Police Authority could now go full-steam ahead, in marketing the land - a prime site attractive to many developers. However, national events were to have an impact on the Police Authority plans.

A banking crisis, no mortgages, businesses going into receivership and the biggest downturn in the building industry anyone could remember resulted in, one by one, developers, who had expressed an interest in purchasing the site, backing out. It soon became clear that in the economic climate the country found itself in, no developer would be willing buy the land.

Time passed and no one seemed to know what was happening until December 2008. The planning permission had by then expired. Stafford Borough Council received notice "that Staffordshire Police were to proceed with the demolition of the following buildings:

Phase 1
Baswich House - 3 storey Victorian House
Crime Block - 4 storey office building
Stores Block - 2 storey office/stores building
Houses at Baswich House Drive - Semi-detached 1960's houses

The Stores Block

Phase 2
Houses at Baswich House Way (No's 1-4) Detached 1960's houses
Weeping Cross Houses (No's 16 - 18 and 22 -32) Detached Semi-detached houses and 2 bungalows.

It is our intention to provisionally commence work on site on Monday, 19th January, 2009."

As with the previous notice to demolish the kennels, the Police Authority's statutory 6 week notice ran over the Christmas and New Year period, thus minimizing the effective time for objections.

---

[59] Built following the fire at the school in 1926

The disturbing stories of misuse of the building continued to emanate from Police Headquarters. There were many tales of the building being used for training dogs, for anti-terrorist manoeuvres, and siege exercises. It was suggested that one developer was prepared to buy the land once Baswich House had been demolished. No-one would speak openly about the misuse of the building but, as time passed, more and more stories emerged.

Now the local press became interested and, slowly, news of the imminent demolition became a major topic of conversation in the area.

Baswich House just prior to demolition

Chapter 17
Fight to the End

Public anger had increased and, as a result, the Leader of Stafford Borough Council, Mrs Judith Dalgarno, requested a meeting with Michael Poulter, the Chairman of the Police Authority. This was arranged for Monday, 2nd February 2009, at 10.30 a.m. It was a bitterly cold day with snow on the ground.

As the time of the meeting approached, members of the public, Berkswich Parish Council, and environmental groups gathered outside Police Headquarters. The Chief Constable, Mr Chris Simms, arrived for work. With a pleasant "Good Morning", he disappeared into the building. A few moments later the receptionist came out to ask what everyone was doing there. As the visit was legitimate, everyone was invited to enter the building and wait.

Soon they were joined by Mrs Dalgarno, Mike Heenan her deputy, the Chief Executive of Stafford Borough Ian Thompson, Jeremy Lefroy, prospective parliamentary candidate for Stafford, a press photographer and Jack Barber, Labour County Councillor for the area.

All had to sign the Visitors Book stating who they were and who they represented before being awarded a badge to be worn whilst in the building. Just before 10.30 Michael Poulter arrived wearing, as always, his trademark bow tie. He was only expecting the Leader of the Council and her Deputy. A quick look around at this noisy mass of people and he retreated out of the door he had just come through.

A little while later he emerged from inside the building, having gained entry from another door. He requested that everyone should follow him. However, during the preceding weekend, John Francis, with a little help from others, had been busy collecting signatures for a petition requesting that Baswich House be saved and used for affordable

Cllr John Francis presents the petition to Michael Poulter

housing. There was to be the little ceremonial act of presenting the petition to the Chairman of the Police Authority, in the presence of the press photographer, before the formal part of the meeting commenced. Those present were in no doubt that, given more time, many more signatures could have been added to the 364 already collected in less than 48 hours.

Following this short ceremony, a crocodile of representatives followed Mr Poulter outside and into the adjoining block, to Conference Room 4 where the smell of coffee permeated the room. Around the table sat the Chairman's support group, David Pearsall (Vice-Chairman), Ralph Butler (Head of Support Services), Mrs D. Talent (Property Development Manager), and Richard Gough of Gough Planning Services.

Mrs Dalgarno was somewhat surprised to find that the meeting was not to be held in Baswich House itself. An immediate re-action from all those representing the Police Authority was that the building was unsafe!

After everyone had introduced themselves and signed the attendance book, Mr Gough outlined the Police Authority's position, stating that "Immediately prior to an Enquiry into the non determination (of the Planning Application), the Borough Council had been advised by their barrister that they had no chance of winning the appeal. A deal was reached with the Borough Council not to defend the appeal but the Police Authority made no demand for the £40,000 costs to be met by the Borough Council".[60]

Why is it that when things come to court it is often a matter of money which finally influences the result?

Mr Gough continued that "there had originally been 10 bidders for the north side of the site but because of the economic climate all bids were down on market value so in Autumn 2008 the Police Authority made the decision not to dispose of the site until market conditions had improved to maximise on income. In the interests of liability and concern of trespass it had then been decided for the police to demolish buildings and clear the site".[61] Mr Poulter then asked for comments from those present.

Remains of Stun Grenades and Training Bullets pictured in Baswich House during demolition

---

[60] Minutes of meeting, 2nd February, 2009
[61] Minutes of meeting, 2nd February, 2009

It was obvious that local people had a great love of the building, which was an outstanding landmark in the area. Comments were made about the loss, over the years, of many of Stafford's lovely buildings, including the Alexandra Hotel, the Station Hotel, and Dale's shop. Pleas were made for the building to be "mothballed" until such time as the land was sold. The decision would then rest with the developer and the Planning Authority as to whether the building would be used, or demolished. This would be in line with the decision of the Planning Inspector.

When asked about the use of Baswich House in recent times, Ralph Butler admitted that the building had been used for periodic fire-arms training in a mock-up situation but, when asked if those present might view the property from the inside, he stated that he would have severe health and safety issues about access, and that the first and second floors were "unsafe". This was the first indication that both the first and second floors were deemed unsafe. The second floor had been restricted to storage only for many years because there was no second floor fire escape. The first floor had remained in use by the Police Museum until 2007, with no suggestion of any safety issue.

The Chairman summarised by saying that "Baswich House is structurally unsafe and having been quoted a cost of at least £1M to make it structurally safe he felt the Police Authority had a responsibility to landscape the site as buildings are demolished to make it safe and free from vandalism"[62]

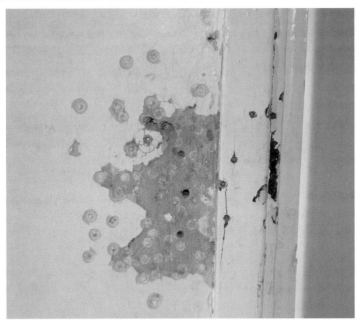

A door frame in Baswich House, peppered with shot

---

[62] Minutes of meeting , 2nd February, 2009

When was the decision to demolish the buildings taken? This question was put to the Chair as no record of this decision had appeared in the Police Authority minutes on the internet. David Pearsall replied saying that he was Chair of the Property Working Group and all meetings were minuted. Michael Poulter intervened saying that the minutes were a public document and the decision was in the public domain. The minutes were readily available and would be provided for inspection. A look of horror crossed the face of David Pearsall. In due course it became clear why he was unhappy about the Chairman's statement.

The minutes were not in the public domain. The decision had been taken by the Property Members/Officers Group on 4th June 2008. These minutes had been deliberately "made exempt from publication by virtue of Paragraph 3 of Part 1 of Schedule 12A of the Local Government Act, 1972[63] and the public interest not to disclose the information outweighs the public interest in disclosing it". The meeting was attended by David Pearsall, Adrian Bowen, Councillors Michael Poulter and Terry Dix, together with ten officers of the Police Authority. It was resolved "that pending improvements in the robustness of the housing market generally, and in the Stafford area, it is in the best interests of the Authority to defer for the time being further progress in marketing the part of the Cannock Road Headquarters site previously identified for disposal, and that in consequence steps be put in hand to demolish all buildings now surplus to Force needs thereon in order to minimise vandalism and safety risks and improve the site appearance". There was no specific mention of Baswich House; it had become just "a building surplus to Force needs".

The proceedings closed with Michael Poulter agreeing to consider the comments made during the meeting. Once in the car park outside it was clear that many of those who were present thought they had been wasting their time. Minds were made up and Baswich House would be demolished.

Following this meeting, Councillor Poulter wrote to the Stafford Newsletter. "We listened very intently and were very impressed by the great interest and commitment so eloquently expressed in its (Baswich House) continued existence. Given the Police Authority's need to withdraw from the care of Baswich House, we thought we should offer the full care and responsibility for it to the Borough Council, should it wish to safeguard the building. We thus sent a letter to Councillor Dalgarno outlining that offer. Failing any such commitment from the Council, the decision to demolish will be activated for reasons I now outline".

Michael Poulter went on to talk about spending money on providing an effective and efficient police force. He did not mention the many millions of pounds being spent in moving Police Headquarters to the Weston Road or the money wasted on recent work carried out on buildings that were shortly to be demolished.

On 3rd February Alan Wallis, Chief Executive of the Police Authority wrote to Councillor Dalgarno outlining the conditions they wished the Borough Council to comply with if Baswich House was to be saved. He asked if the Borough Council was "prepared to :-

1.   *Wholly fund the erection of appropriate security fencing around Baswich House to a specification and standard on which the Police Authority and the Borough*

---

[63] Information relating to the financial or business affairs of any particular person (including the authority holding that information)

Council are agreed: and to meet all costs associated with the maintenance thereafter of such fencing to that standard;

2. (a) Accept full responsibility for, and fully indemnify the Police Authority against all and any public liabilities (including all costs claims and damages) which may arise from the retention of Baswich House, including those associated with the liability of an occupier to a trespasser, with confirmation now and for each subsequent year from the Borough Council's insurers as to the existence of insurance cover in respect of the foregoing indemnity, and against such liabilities, in a sum of not less than £10M;

(b) Carry out such care and maintenance of Baswich House as may be necessary in the opinion of the Borough Council to minimise any risks for which liability could arise under paragraph 2 (a) above, but not imposing any obligation to improve the condition of the property from its current state.

3. Charge a nil Business Rate for the building for so long as it remains in the legal ownership of the Police Authority.

4. (a) Indemnify the Police Authority against all costs incurred by the Authority arising from the withdrawal of Baswich House from the current demolition contract for the properties at the north end of the Cannock Road site.

(b)   Indemnify the Police Authority against the cost of the demolition of Baswich House should the property be demolished at any time while it remains in the ownership of the Police Authority.

As you will appreciate, the Police Authority is eager to resolve this matter and the response of the Borough Council is required within 28 days of the date of this letter. If no response is forthcoming, or the Borough Council is unwilling or unable to enter into the appropriate arrangements necessary to remove in full from the Police Authority any financial burden associated with the retention of the building, the demolition of Baswich House must proceed."

Two days later Councillor Dalgarno responded to the Police Authority letter. *"This letter reads as an ultimatum and is not in tone the sort of communication I would expect to receive between authorities who have established a working partnership for the benefit of the community."*

Referring to the meeting held on 2nd February she says *"At no time was a suggestion made that the Borough Council would take over financial responsibility for this building and it is disingenuous for you to suggest this since no doubt you would wish to retain any proceeds of sale of the building when ultimately sold for development. Para 4 (b) also seeks to pass the cost of demolition of the building to the Borough Council, in the event of a developer not being able to incorporate it in their plans.*

Mrs Judith Dalgarno

Our offer of discussions over fencing and rates between our two authorities was made in a spirit of partnership working and remain on the table for you to consider. It was not a licence for you to try and offload your responsibilities in this matter.

It is up to you to decide in the light of representations made and our helpful offer whether you wish to attempt to save this building for future generations".

At its meeting on 26th February Stafford Borough Council considered the proposals put to them by the Police Authority. After a lengthy debate the Council resolved (a) that this Council requests the Police Authority to reconsider its decision to demolish Baswich House immediately and to consider incorporating the building into any proposed development; (b) that the Council agrees to investigate ways it can contribute towards making the building safe and secure.

Whilst the Borough Council were prepared to provide some financial assistance towards protecting the building until such time as the housing market recovered and the land could be sold, they were not in a position to agree to the unreasonable financial demands made by the Police Authority.

Did the Police Authority as a whole reconsider its decision as requested by Stafford Borough Council? No! The Authority had held a meeting on 11th February when the Petition was formally presented to them. At that meeting the power to take any further action regarding Baswich House was passed to the Chief Executive (Alan Wallis) in consultation with the Chair (Michael Poulter) and the Vice-Chair (David Pearsall) of the Authority. It would appear that the final decision on the fate of Baswich House was left in the hands of these three men, only one of whom was an elected representative of the people.

Debris left behind in Baswich House - including a Programme to celebrate 150th Anniversary of Staffordshire Police!

Chapter 18
Bats & Things

Letters poured into the Press in support of keeping Baswich House. They came not just from local people in Weeping Cross, but from much further afield, from Gnosall, Cannock, Woodseaves, Burton on Trent, and the Isle of Wight,[64] along with emails of support and telephone calls from Dorset and Sussex. It appeared that only two people were prepared to publicly back Michael Poulter. Both were Labour Councillors, viz Mr Michael Millichap and Ralph Cooke (who had been a neighbour of the Poulter family when they lived in Brunswick Terrace).

The supporters of Baswich House made every effort to prevent the demolition going ahead. If bats were found in the house, it would not prevent the demolition but it could certainly slow things down. County Council elections were due in June and perhaps, if things could be delayed until after then, there might be a change in administration and also in attitude.[65]

All British bat species are afforded protection under the Wildlife and Countryside Act 1981. This legislation makes it illegal to kill, injure, capture bats, or to obstruct access to, damage or destroy bat roosts. A bat roost is interpreted as any place used for shelter or protection whether or not bats are present at the time. The penalty for breaking the law is a fine of up to £5000 (per bat disturbed/killed) and up to six months imprisonment.

Had the Bat survey been completed as the Inspector had requested in his formal decision on the Planning Inquiry?

In August 2003 CSa Environmental Planning had undertaken an Ecological Appraisal on behalf of Staffordshire Police which had been submitted with the Planning Application.

This Appraisal states:- "Bats. The Buildings on the site are of varying ages, but are all in relatively good state of repair. Some of these have a greater potential as bat roosting habitats than others. Baswich House, the large Victorian building in the southwest corner of the site, has particular potential, although the more modern buildings could also be suitable. All the buildings have tiled roofs (with the exception of the modern three storey building with the lead roof), which tend to provide access points for bats when they slip or break, creating gaps".[66]

CSa Environmental Planning expected to find bats in and around Baswich House. Letters from local residents stated that there were bats flying round the area. Walk around the area at dusk and bats could be seen swooping around regularly. They had to roost somewhere close by.

In June and July 2008 CSa were requested to undertake a bat survey of the planning application site at Police Headquarters in line with the Planning Inspector's demands. Things were now very different. CSa had changed their opinion, following their survey.

---

[64] Some of these letters are reproduced in the appendix at the end of the book.
[65] At the County Council Elections on 4th June, 2009, the Labour Party was decimated and left with only 3 Labour Councillors in the whole county
[66] Environmental Appraisal Page 10 Para 4.12

Three surveys were undertaken on 24th June, 3rd July and 16th July. On two occasions there were three surveyors watching for bat activity over the whole site. On 16th July, four surveyors were employed to cover the site. Bats were definitely around.

Remember that in 2003 Csa Environmental Planning had said that "Baswich House has particular potential" for bats to roost. Now we find that they were unable to complete a full internal survey of the house. The survey states "Certain areas of Baswich House to the southeast of the building were unsafe to walk on so could not therefore be internally inspected. These areas were however assessed thoroughly from the exterior and observed carefully during the activity surveys."

The team did however, gain access to part of the building. The survey goes on to say "Access opportunities (for the bats) into the building are provided by loose roof tiles and open windows. Further access and roosting opportunities are provided by gaps under lead flashing. No evidence of bats was seen on the exterior of the building". The report, after describing the dusty, draughty conditions in the roof space, eventually admits to finding "very old (over 10 years old) droppings which were unidentifiable in a loft space towards the north of Baswich House, no evidence of bats was found anywhere in this building".

The layman may like to ask two questions. Firstly, how long does it take for a bat dropping to disintegrate? Ten years is a very long time for a very small item to decompose. Secondly, would the barking of dogs, the firing of ammunition and the shouts of Police Officers, as they practise their anti-terrorist tactics, do anything to encourage any bats to make their home in Baswich House? We will never know. We do

Pipistrelle Bat in the palm of the hand.

know however, that bats were found in some of the 1960's houses.

Letters continued to flood into the local newspapers and, time and time again, Michael Poulter was reported as saying the building was dangerous, that the Health & Safety Executive had insisted that the site be vacated, and that it would take £1M to make it safe.

The Health & Safety Executive had had enough. They were tired of reading incorrect reports. They contacted Gail Atkinson, a reporter on the "Stafford Newsletter", keen to put the record straight. A spokesman said "Following an investigation in 2001 we agreed with the course of action to relocate staff from Baswich House by the end of 2001. We went in as a result of an accident and the authority was already in the process of moving people out.

A risk assessment showed there were some aspects of the working environment which made the environment unsafe but it doesn't make the building unsafe".

However, this revelation had come too late. Final plans for the demolition had been completed. Work was to start on Monday 9th March.

Part of the Staircase on the "Dump"

One last attempt had been made to prevent the demolition going ahead. A Stafford resident wrote an urgent letter to the Chief Constable, Chris Simms, asking him to halt the start of the destruction scheduled for the following day. He tried to deliver it by hand on Sunday evening, so that it would be on the Chief's desk first thing on Monday morning. There was no letter-box at Headquarters! The letter had to be posted. An email copy was sent, but to no avail. The following morning a telephone call to his office revealed that the Chief Constable was on leave, preparing for his forthcoming interview for the post of Chief Constable of the West Midlands[67] and that there were no executive officers at Headquarters that day [or the following day] & no senior officers were available to speak to him.

What about the Chairman of the Police Authority? Was he available? No, he was on his way to London to receive his M.B.E. for services to the community!

---

[67] Chris Simms was appointed Chief Constable of the West Midlands, the authority from which he had come just 18 months previously.

Perhaps the Chief Executive of the Police Authority was available? No, he was on leave in France!

The contractors moved in, no one was prepared to stop work going ahead, and gradually the building was stripped of its panelling, carved fireplaces and beautiful doors.

Although on police property and surrounded by security fencing, Baswich House, over the following three weeks, was visited on a regular basis by several Staffordshire residents. Within days of the start of demolition, internal photographs appeared on the internet showing that although the house had been neglected and misused by the police authority, it was not in a dangerous state.

Chris Simms, Chief Constable of Staffordshire, during the demolition of Baswich House

The president of the national conservation charity, "Save Britain's Heritage", Marcus Binney said of the demolition, "it is a disgraceful example of the needless destruction of public property by a public authority."

Baswich House, March 2009

Chapter 19
Finale

At the County Council Elections in June 2009 Michael Poulter lost his seat representing Stafford West on the County Council. In the 2005 elections he had polled 3,658 votes. In 2009, this crashed to 1,286 and he was comfortably defeated. He, therefore, was no longer eligible to be a Member of Staffordshire Police Authority.

The Police Authority submitted an outline planning application to Stafford Borough Council in June 2009 for permission to build 200 houses on the whole Police Headquarters site. The original planning application had been for only 80 houses on part of the site.

At the Annual General Meeting of the Police Authority on 21St July, 2009, David Pearsall, the former Vice-Chairman, was elected Chairman in Michael Poulter's place. Mr Pearsall had not had to submit himself to the wrath of the local community because he was an "independent" member of the Police Authority, nominated to the Authority by his fellow magistrates!

Window from Baswich House

On Wednesday, 2nd December, 2009, the planning application submitted by the Police Authority to Stafford Borough Council in June was considered by the Development Control Sub-committee. At this meeting outline permission was granted for development on the site of Baswich House. The trees are protected by Tree Preservation Orders which means that only 5 hectares of the site will be available for development. Councillors expressed their concern about increased traffic in the area. They were also anxious to see the telecommunication mast removed.

Baswich House remains a memory. We do however have some reminders of the building. In February, 2009, two members of Berkswich History Society were given permission by the Police Authority to enter the ground floor only of Baswich House and take photographs. Restrictions have been placed on the Society which prevent us using any of the photographs in this book, despite a request to the Authority to lift these restrictions now that the demolition is complete and irreversible.

With the cooperation of the demolition gang we obtained two small windows as a memento of the building. Maybe others have gathered souvenirs of Baswich House from among the rubble and somewhere, someone may be sitting in a room surrounded by the oak panelling taken from the dining room!

The Weeping Cross Salt Family Tree

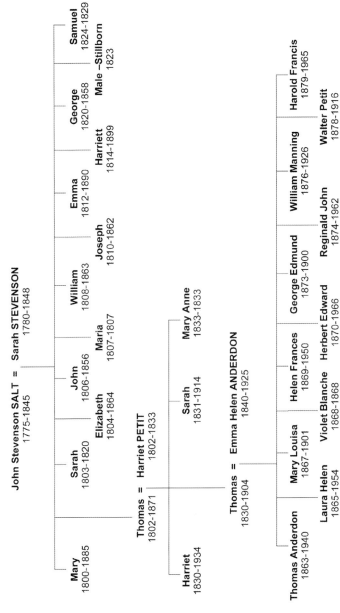

Appendix 2

Census Returns for Weeping Cross House 1841 - 1911

1841 Census   7th June, 1841

Thomas Salt	39	Banker	Not born in Staffs.
Harriett Salt	11		Staffs
Sarah Salt	9		Staffs
Charlotte Huntington	38	Governess	Not born in Staffs
Thomas Grant	24	Man Servant	Staffs
Sarah Bailey	50	Servant	Staffs
Mary West	35	Servant	Staffs
Ann Hearock	25	Servant	Staffs
Margaret Hemmings	22	Servant	Staffs

1851 Census   30th March, 1851

Thomas Salt	49	Widow	Banker	Middlesex, St Pancras
Harriett Salt	20	Daughter		Stafford, Weeping Cross
Sarah Salt	19	Daughter		Stafford, Weeping Cross
Mary Anlezack	23	Visitor	Clergyman's Daughter	Stafford, Castle Church
Mary Rochford	36	Servant	Housekeeper	Staffs. Froghall
Ann Icke	28	Servant	Lady's Maid	Salop. High Ercall
Elizabeth Smith	34	Servant	House Maid	Staffs. Rugeley
Emma Pershouse	18	Servant	Kitchen Maid	Stafford. Weeping Cross
Richard Smith	18	Visitor	Banker's Clerk	Derby. Repton
William Beech	34	Servant	Coachman	Staffs. Burntwood
James Glover	19	Servant	Footman	Staffs. Ranton

1861 Census   7th April, 1861

Name	Age	Relation	Occupation	Birthplace
Thomas Salt	59	Widow	Banker & Landowner	Middlesex London
Thomas Salt	30	Son	Banker & MP	Staffs. Baswich
Elizabeth Hassall	33	Servant	Housekeeper, Dom. Servant	Salop. Albrighton
Henry Whitefoot	40	Servant	Butler, Dom. Servant	Salop. Donnington
William Bullock	18	Servant	Groom, Dom. Servant	Staffs. Lichfield
Ann Cheadle	18	Servant	Kitchen Maid Dom. Servant	Staffs. Colwich

1871 Census   2nd April, 1871

[Thomas Salt Senior had died on 21st March. Resident in Weeping Cross House were the following servants]

Name	Age	Relation	Occupation	Birthplace
Thomas Baker	27	Servant	Butler	Ticehurst (E. Sussex)
Henry Speed	18	Servant	Groom	Bradley
Caroline Wetherby	44	Servant	Housekeeper	Uxbridge
Sarah Hartwell	27	Servant	Cook	Elford, Staffordshire

Sarah Salt was resident at the Inns of Court Hotel, in London.
Thomas Salt Junior was still at his home in Walton on the Hill, see below.

Name	Age	Relation	Occupation	Birthplace
Thomas Salt	40	Head	Income from dividends, M.P., J.P., D.L., Landowner	Stafford. Weeping Cross
Emma H.M. Salt	31	Wife		London
Helen Francis Salt	4	Daughter		Staffs. Walton on the Hill, Baswich
Herbert Edward Salt	4 months	Son		Staffs. Walton on the Hill, Baswich
Mary Hemmings	27	Servant	Cook, Domestic Servant	Staffs. Walton in Baswich
Margaret Powell	26	Servant	Housemaid	Brecon South Wales
Annie Cockram	32	Servant	Nurse (Married)	Woolwich
Elizabeth Clowes	34	Servant	Nurse (Married)	Leicestershire, Ribworth
Emma Pye	14	Servant	Under Nurse	Staffs. Weeping Cross, Baswich
Hannah Hessey	19	Servant	Under Housemaid	Uxbridge
Mary Rigby	20	Servant	Lady's Maid	Notts. Ilkeston (Sic)

1881 Census   3rd April, 1881

[Following his defeat at the 1880 General Election, Thomas, his wife and his 4 older children travelled abroad and therefore do not appear in the 1881 Census.]

George b. 1873 and Reginald b. 1874 were at a Boys School in Eaton Place, Brighton.
William b.1876, Walter b.1878 and Harold b. 1879 were being cared for by a Nurse in Clevedon, Somerset, close to their Aunt Harriet.
Herbert b 1870 was a pupil at St Mark's School, in Windsor.

1891 Census   5th April, 1891

Thomas Salt	60	Head	MP, Director, Joint Stock Co.	Berkswich, Stafford
Emma H.M. Salt	51	Wife		St Pancras
Herbert Edward Salt	21	Son	University Student	Walton Staffordshire
Helen F. Salt	22	Daughter	Maintained by her father	Walton, Staffordshire
Walter Salt	12	Son	Scholar	Berkswich, Staffs.
Irene Elland Harlander	71	Sister in Law	Living on her own income	New Street, Spring Gardens London
Mary Julia Fulford	40	Visitor	Living on her own income	St Mary Staffordshire
Louisa Fanny Madan	26	Visitor	Maintained by her brother	Standon, Staffs
Emma Flinch	39	Visitor	Sister of Mercy - Nun	Henley on Thames, Oxon
John Beech	12	Servant	Footman Dom. Servant	Castle Church, Stafford
Samuel Slow	20	Servant	Footman Dom Ser.	Worcestershire
William Arlott	22	Servant	Groom (Stable Groom)	Silchester, Hants
?? Sillock	43	Servant	Butler	Cottsmore, Rutland (Sic)
Marion ???	37	Servant	Housemaid	Bath, Somerset
Mary E. Clewes	20	Servant	Housemaid	Castle Church, Stafford
Esther Brigham	16	Servant	Kitchenmaid	Hastings
Mary Wiffen?	45	Servant	Housekeeper	Edi???, Middlesex

1901 Census   31st March, 1901

Name	Age	Role	Occupation	Location
Thomas Salt	70	Head	Living on own means	Staffs. Baswich
Emma H.M. Salt	61	Wife		London, Marylebone
Mary Lavies	34	Daughter	Widow, Living on own means	Staffs. Berkswich
Emmanuel Purchouse	59	Servant	Butler	Somerset, Hardington Manderville
John Beech	20	Servant	Footman	Stafford
Susan Grainger	49	Servant	Lady's Maid	At sea (Nr Island of St Helena British Subject)
Annie M. ??land	44	Servant	Housemaid	Kent, Kennington
Henrietta Peace	19	Servant	Kitchenmaid	Staffs. Lichfield
Edith Newill	19	Servant	Housemaid	Staffs. Wolverhampton
Mary Balkin	18	Servant	Housemaid	Staffs. Stafford
Clare Astle	16	Servant	Scullerymaid	Staffs, Histon (Stowe)
Harriett Fletcher	23	Servant	Lady's maid	Kent Lynshed
Cassie L. Barker	31	Sick Nurse	Professional Nurse	Northants. Peterborough.

1911 Census 2nd April, 1911

In 1911 William Morton Philips and his family were in London.

How they voted at the 1869 General Election

ANALYSIS OF THE POLL.

Qualification of Voters	No. on Register	SPLIT VOTES						PLUMPERS				No. Polled	Duplicates	Dead	Unpolled
		Salt and Talbot	Evans and Whitworth	Salt and Evans	Salt and Whitworth	Talbot and Evans	Talbot and Whitworth	Salt	Talbot	Evans	Whitworth				
Freemen . . .	1017	491	350	13	7	2	1	8	1	1	1	875	37	20	85
Householders, St. Mary & St. Chad	1613	396	405	18	13	—	3	8	—	3	3	849	485	31	248
Lodgers, ditto .	6	3	2	1	—	—	—	—	—	—	—	6	—	—	—
Householders, Castle Church	511	227	151	8	3	—	1	5	1	—	1	397	28	15	71
Lodgers, ditto .	5	3	1	—	—	—	—	—	—	—	—	4	—	—	1
Total	3152	1120	909	40	23	2	5	21	2	4	5	2131	550	66	405

Appendix 4

Chief Constables of Staffordshire
1952 - 2009

The following officers have been responsible for the care and management of Baswich House whilst it has been occupied by Staffordshire Police.

Colonel George Hearn, 1951 - 1960

Mr Stanley Peck, 1960 - 1964

Mr Arthur Rees, 1964 - 1977

Mr Charles Kelly, 1977 - 1996

Mr John Giffard, 1996 - March 2006

Mr David Swift, April 2006 - June 2007

Mr Chris Simms, July 2007 - April 2009

Appendix 5

The Cost of Demolishing Baswich House and other Buildings
Information provided by the Chief Executive of Staffordshire Police Authority,
Mr Alan Wallis, on 19th March, 2009

The demolition work was tendered for an entire phase of the demolition which included the Stores Block, Baswich House, the six houses on Baswich House Drive and the former Crime Block. The total tendered costs are:

DSM (main demolition contractor) - £108,640 tendered.

Pectel (Midlands) Ltd (Asbestos Removal) - estimated at £38,465 based on Schedule of Rates (which prices for the various component activities, rather than as an overall figure, so that the Authority only pays for the actual work necessary in connection with asbestos removal).

Environmental Essentials (Monitoring of Asbestos Removal) - estimated at £8,500 based on Schedule of Rates (which prices for the various component activities, rather than as an overall figure, so that the Authority only pays for the actual work necessary in connection with the monitoring of asbestos removal).

Total £155,605

How much would it have cost to secure all doors and windows in Baswich House until such time as a developer could be found for the site?

Letters

The following are extracts from some of the many letters published in the local press during the early months of 2009.

The Photographs in the *Newsletter* of Baswich House, this attractive old building, bring back memories of wartime schooldays at Stafford Girls High School when we had lessons there every Tuesday and Thursday, while evacuees from Ramsgate used the Oval. For us the exchange gave us an exciting peep into the past with its carved wood interior and extensive grounds to explore.

It is unbelievable that this historic house should die of neglect after surviving for more than 150 years when it has the potential to serve the community in so many ways.

The Council might consider conversion into flats to rent to those who, through no fault of their own in the present recession, find themselves jobless and homeless.

However this would prove expensive and require major reconstruction. A more fitting and less damaging change of use would be to adapt it as a county museum, something that Stafford lacks. A blue plaque might record that Sir Thomas Salt lived there, MP for Stafford from 1859 to 1892.

A comprehensive museum tracing the history of Stafford would raise public awareness of the need to preserve our heritage. School children especially would benefit from museum visits and hopefully grow up aware of the need for vigilance in guarding against the destruction of historic assets for short term monetary gain.

******

Here we go again, yet another fight is on to save an historic building in Stafford, this time round it's the undeniably beautiful Baswich House. This building despite it lasting over 150 years, will be bulldozed all in the name of "development".

The classic quote from county councillor Mike Poulter stating "If we leave any buildings they will be subject to vandalism and deterioration. In the interests of the local population we have to leave the site in good repair" was laughable and utter waffle. We're led to believe it's the only way for development to occur and that way is, to knock down whatever stands in the developer's way and also, if we leave a building long enough, it's rendered useless. Would he also back the idea of Stafford Castle being demolished to make way for housing?

******

OK, I'm sure Baswich House has had a few adjustments in its history but this only adds to the overall look of the building.

We're not talking about a two bed semi-detached built in the 1970's that had a dodgy extension in the '80's and a plastic conservatory added in the '90's.

This is a building full of history and also a building that gives us a dramatic and impressive exterior. I'm sure that if anything does replace it, then that development will warrant no architectural merit whatsoever (as we've seen before to other "yes-we-should-have-kept-them" buildings)

I'm not quite sure we would be trying to save Baswich House's replacement in 100 years time, are you?

*****

Why on earth would you want to demolish a lovely 150 year old building to put up "cardboard houses"?

The council are looking to spend £23 million on new offices yet there's nothing wrong with the old ones. They're just too lazy to walk to another building to get to another department. Why not save some of this £23 million they're about to waste and refurbish the buildings they currently use, and refurbish Baswich House?

How they can use vandals as an excuse to get rid of it I do not know, it's been standing there going to waste for several years and has not been or hardly vandalised so why would that change now?

******

So, now Cllr Mike Poulter has had his wish come true, Baswich House has been razed to the ground. What an utter disgrace for the people and town of Stafford. A building that has stood for 160 years has been demolished with the support of a Labour County Councillor – who in the same month received the MBE for his community work, and is also a trustee of the William Salt Library.

How can a Police Authority (a public funded body paid for by our rates) operate in such a way as to disregard public opinion on this matter? The decision to relocate the Police HQ to the Weston Road site beggars belief. The Police HQ in its present commanding position was open to the public as all public bodies should be. Indeed the way the Police HQ and the Staffordshire Police was run 10 or 12 years ago was wonderful compared to today. They had Open Days, the SPACE scheme for young people, a Summer Fête with the horses, dogs, police cars and more. In other words, a marvellous public relations exercise that helped to boost the Police's standing in the community.

What we have now is, NO horses, NO police patrol cars of our own, NO cadets.... it goes on and on, and now a demolished H.Q.

*****

The Leader of the Police Authority has decided to demolish Baswich House, the historic building at Police H.Q. in Stafford. He says the four huge office blocks surrounding Baswich House have also passed their useful life span. The truth is they are only half the age of the Corporation Street houses where he lives. I bet his family do not regard the family home as being past its useful life.

*****

The open letter my friend County Councillor Michael Poulter sent to Borough Councillors last month hardly cooled passions over the fate of Baswich House.

He seems to suggest the Police Authority he chairs had to choose between saving this historic building and putting police officers on the beat. After 28 years of spending taxpayers' money, Cllr Poulter knows that demolishing the 160 year old mansion will not let him employ a single extra police officer. The Authority can sell the site only once, whereas employees' salaries need funding year after year.

In the current economic climate, the chances of a quick sale of the Police Headquarters site, with or without Baswich House standing, are slim.

A period of calm could have lowered the political temperature from its current feverish level and allowed reflection on the options a new owner might find for this landmark which is part of Stafford's historical fabric.

Now, Cllr Poulter may find the political price he had to pay for sending in the bulldozers before polling day on June 4th is very high indeed.

*****

The Press have had a field day revealing the expenses of our MP's. Our eyes have been opened. Perhaps with the event of County Council elections on 4th June we should look at the Councillors in and around Stafford who are putting themselves forward for re-election. Have they done a done a good job? Do they deserve the payments they receive?

A request for information about the expenses of the Police Authority was turned down because "some members are not elected representatives". I am sure that we would still like to know how our money is being spent. One thing however, that is publicly available, is that Michael Poulter, receives £25,123 as Chairman of the Police Authority plus £143.50 p.a. for telephone expenses. His Vice-Chairman, David Pearsall, whom I must add is not an elected representative, receives £21,031.

While on the subject of Baswich House I must commend Wolverhampton City Council for its protection of an old building. The Molineux Hotel, close to the "Wolves" ground was originally the home of the Molineux family before becoming an hotel. The hotel closed in the late 1970's and began to fall into disrepair. In 2003 the building caught fire, following which it was bought by the City Council and has been restored to its former glory. The building is now the Wolverhampton Archives and Local Studies Centre with fantastic facilities, car parking, and gardens all close to the city centre. This site would no doubt have been worth many millions of pounds to a developer but the Council had the foresight to protect a wonderful building for posterity.

The Mayor of Stafford at the time of the Baswich House demolition, Mrs Ann Edgeller, lived close to Police Headquarters. One day she asked the Demolition Gang where the panelling and fireplaces had gone. She was told that they "had gone to London".

In an attempt to find exactly where the panelling would end up a letter was sent to the Demolition Company, DSM Demolition Ltd, Birmingham saying *"Berkswich History Society is in the process of writing a book about the history of the house and the people who have lived and worked in it from 1840 until early this year. In order to complete the final chapter of the book we would like to be able to record where the reclaimed panelling/staircase and fireplaces have ended up. It would be great if they have found a home in some other historical house.*

I would be grateful if you could inform me where these items have ended their days, or if they are still available for sale."

After a month the following reply was received. *"In response to your letter dated 16th April, 2009, I write to confirm that 90.5% by volume of the buildings recently demolished at the above mentioned site have been recycled and fed back into the construction supply chain".*

It does not answer the question!

Acknowledgements

We wish to extend our thanks to the following people. Without their help this book would not have been possible.

Sir Michael Salt who provided paintings, photographs, and information that have added greatly to this book.

Thea Randall, Staffordshire County Archivist, for her support and for permission to use photographs and paintings belonging to the William Salt Library and Staffordshire Record Office.

All the Staff of the William Salt Library and the Staffordshire County Record Office for their patience and assistance.

Randle W. Knight for pointing us in the right directions on several occasions.

Neil Hatfield, Archivist to the Philips family.

Jennifer Lewis & The Lewis Family Collection for use of several pictures of Baswich House School & Sale Documents 1915.

We acknowledge the use of the Staffordshire Advertiser and Staffordshire Chronicle during our research.

Many other members of the public who have shared their memories or loaned photographs for use in this book, including – Richard Browne, Rob. Campbell, Glynis Connolly, Beatrice Hall, Trevor Houlton, Joy Lewis, Muriel Lightfoot, Peter and Jane Nunn, J. Peters, Christopher Phillips, Henry Teasdale, Joan Tyldesley, Alan Walker, Jean Wooster.

The following members of Berkswich History Society have all been involved in one way or another in the production of this book –
Jean Alden, Nadia Davies, Dorothy Keeling, Kevin Kelly,
Beryl and John Holt, Dorothy Johnson, Robin and Anne Landon,
Robert Morton, Valerie Peach, Muriel Scott,
F.J. and J. Vaughan, Martin Woollaston.

INDEX OF PEOPLE